PLAY
ROCK
GUITAR

DK

DORLING KINDERSLEY
London • New York • Stuttgart • Moscow

CONTENTS

WHAT DO YOU NEED?

AN ELECTRIC GUITAR, an amplifier, and three or four simple chords have been at the heart of many of the best-known rock groups. One of the great things about learning to play rock guitar is that you can quickly achieve a very familiar sound – plug in an electric guitar for the first time, turn up the volume, distort the sound, and within minutes you will feel as if you have just joined the Velvet Underground.

Fender Stratocaster

HOW TO USE THE BOOK AND CD

To use this package, the minimum requirement is a guitar, an amplifier, and a CD player (one with a remote control will make life easier). The first part of the book concentrates simply on learning the guitar – these lessons can be applied equally well to an acoustic guitar and an electric guitar. Alongside the examples and exercises you will see a CD symbol. This indicates that you can listen to these examples being played, or play along yourself.

The numbers beside the CD symbol indicate the track and index point on which the exercise can be heard. If you have a CD player that cannot read index points, simply use the pause control on the CD player and it will automatically play the next piece. The second part of the book concentrates more on the sound of the guitar, amplifier, and various effects, using the CD as a guide to the many varied sound possibilities.

 16/3

CD symbol and numbers
The disc indicates music that is on the CD. The numbers are track number/index point.

Vox AC30
Used on some of the best-known recordings by the Beatles and Rolling Stones, the Vox AC30 valve "combo" remains popular over 30 years after it was first produced. A combo is an amplifier and loudspeaker housed in the same cabinet. Some guitarists prefer to use a separate amplifier and speaker cabinet.

CHOOSING A GUITAR

If you are buying an electric guitar for the first time, you will be safer going to an established guitar shop, rather than buying privately. A sensible rule is to buy the best you can afford – it is easy to end up with something cheap but unplayable. Here are some basic considerations:

● CHECK THAT the fingerboard is not warped. Hold the guitar as if it were a rifle, and align your eye with the edge of the neck. If it is bent, the intonation will be poor.

● CHECK THE DISTANCE between the top of the 12th fret and the bottom of the string (the action). If it is more than $1/12$ in (0.2 cm), the guitar will be difficult to play.

● PLAY EVERY NOTE on the fingerboard, listening carefully for the string buzzing against the fret. You should avoid guitars with overly worn frets.

● TURN THE MACHINE HEADS. If they feel too loose, the strings may slip, making the guitar difficult to keep in tune.

● PLUG THE GUITAR into an amplifier and check the relative volume of each string. If there are major variations, have the height of the pickups adjusted.

● TEST THE TONE and volume controls. Adjust them while you play to be sure that they work, and that the sound does not crackle.

● ENSURE THAT THE AMPLIFIER in the shop is not enhancing the quality of the guitar. Ask for any effects to be switched off so that you hear only the amplified guitar.

CHOOSING AN AMPLIFIER

It is always a good idea to take your own guitar when you test an amplifier – this is the only way you will really know if the amplifier is the right piece of equipment for your sound. Before you choose an amplifier, think about what you may want to do with it eventually and how loud you want to be able to play. If you plan to play live performances, you are likely to need between 50 and 100 watts of power. Remember, though, that high output is not always a sign of quality. Take care with amplifiers that offer a lot of additional effects. Make sure that you really need them – some of the best and most popular amplifiers are simple models designed over 30 years ago. Here are some other useful pointers:

- If you buy a second-hand amplifier, avoid models that look too battered – this would indicate that the amplifier has been heavily used or badly treated.
- Listen for excess buzzing or hiss when you are not playing – it may mean that the circuitry is worn or damaged.
- Look at the speaker cone and ensure that it is not torn or dented. This will adversely affect the sound.
- Test all of the controls to ensure that they do what they are supposed to without making crackling noises.
- Stamp your foot on the ground next to the amplifier. If the amplifier crackles, there may be a loose valve or circuitry. This is likely to cause problems eventually.

The complete works
To use this book, all you really need is a guitar, amplifier, and CD player. However, there are a great many other optional pieces of equipment that you can use, some of which are shown here.

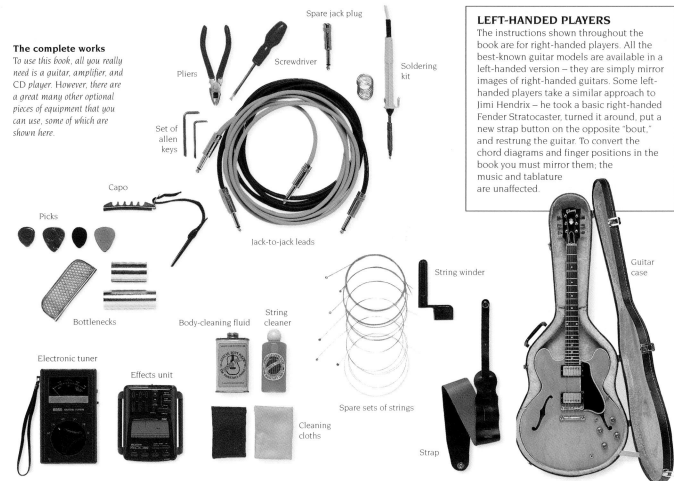

Spare jack plug

Pliers

Screwdriver

Soldering kit

Set of allen keys

Capo

Picks

Jack-to-jack leads

Bottlenecks

Body-cleaning fluid

String cleaner

String winder

Guitar case

Electronic tuner

Effects unit

Spare sets of strings

Cleaning cloths

Strap

LEFT-HANDED PLAYERS

The instructions shown throughout the book are for right-handed players. All the best-known guitar models are available in a left-handed version – they are simply mirror images of right-handed guitars. Some left-handed players take a similar approach to Jimi Hendrix – he took a basic right-handed Fender Stratocaster, turned it around, put a new strap button on the opposite "bout," and restrung the guitar. To convert the chord diagrams and finger positions in the book you must mirror them; the music and tablature are unaffected.

GUITAR HISTORY

THE ORIGINS of the guitar are difficult to trace. While conclusive evidence shows that a figure-of-eight-shaped instrument was used in the 13th century, the precursors of the guitar are thought to date back to Babylonian and ancient Egyptian times. The first recognizable guitars appeared during the Renaissance. Initially, these were considered to be greatly inferior to related stringed instruments such as the lute and vihuela. While similar in appearance to modern day instruments, these early guitars were very much smaller and had four "courses" – sets of doubled strings usually made from sheep's intestines.

Matteo Sellas
This instrument was built in the early 17th century by the prominent luthier Matteo Sellas. The fingerboard has nine frets.

THE CLASSICAL GUITAR

The conventional six-string guitar originated in Italy around 1780. During the middle of the 19th century, the Spanish guitar maker Antonio de Torres Jurado produced a larger instrument, the dimensions and construction of which are still used today.

Towards the end of the 19th century, Francisco Tárrega defined much of what is now considered to be standard classical playing techniques. However, it was perhaps the virtuoso Andrés Segovia who, more than any other, was responsible for the acceptance of the guitar as a valid classical instrument.

THE GUITAR IN THE US

The evolution of the modern guitar largely took place in the US, where two distinct styles developed: the "flat top" and the "arch top." In 1833 a well established German instrument maker, C. F. Martin, settled in the US. The Martin company went on to became one of the world's principal guitar manufacturers, pioneering the flat-top acoustic guitar. The designs that developed during the 1920s,

Antonio de Torres
The Torres design revolutionized the development of the guitar. This instrument dates back to 1860.

Martin OM-28
The Martin "orchestral model" was launched in the late 1920s. Unusually for the time, the neck joined the body at the 14th fret, giving improved access to the upper register.

when steel strings gained prominence over gut, have undergone relatively little change since. They have been widely used by country and rock artists over the years.

Orville Gibson began to manufacture his own instruments at the end of the 19th century. Gibson, having studied the way in which violins were made, pioneered the arch-top design, where the body of the instrument was curved rather than flat. The Gibson company was later at the forefront of developments in the field of amplified guitars.

THE EARLY ELECTRICS

By the 1920s guitars were being used commonly in jazz and dance bands. Because of their relatively low volume, they were generally used only to provide rhythmic backing. In an attempt to solve this problem, one of Gibson's engineers, Lloyd Loar, began to experiment with the use of electronic pickups. It was, however, another American company, Rickenbacker, who in

Rickenbacker Electro Spanish
Introduced in 1931, the Electro Spanish is generally recognized as the first electric guitar to have been manufactured commercially.

1931 made the first commercially available electronic stringed instrument – the "Frying Pan" lap steel guitar. A year later they introduced the first commercially available electric guitar – the Electro Spanish. This was a basic arch-top design fitted with a horseshoe magnet pickup. It was the Gibson ES-150, launched a few years afterwards, that captured the imagination of jazz guitarist Charlie Christian, who largely established the electric guitar as a serious musical proposition.

THE SOLID BODY

A fundamental problem resulted from fitting electronic pickups to an acoustic guitar. If the amplifier volume was too great, the sound from the loudspeaker would cause the body of the guitar to vibrate, creating a howling noise, or "feedback." The solution was to increase the body mass of the instrument to reduce vibration. So, in the 1940s, the first solid-body

electric guitars appeared. There is a good deal of controversy as to who produced the first solid-body guitar. Guitarist Les Paul created his own "Log" guitar using a Gibson neck attached to a solid piece of pine on which the pickups and bridge were mounted. Paul used the Log on many of his hit records.

Another claimant to the title was engineer Paul Bigsby, who produced a solid-body electric guitar for the country guitarist Merle Travis. The shape and construction of this guitar had a direct influence on Leo Fender, subsequently the most influential maker of solid-body electric guitars. In 1950 Leo Fender's California, USA-based company launched the first mass-market, solid-body electric guitar – the Fender Broadcaster. The following year it was renamed the Telecaster. In 1954 he produced the legendary Stratocaster guitar. In 1952 the Gibson company launched the Les Paul solid-body.

Gibson ES-175

One of the first electric guitars to be manufactured on a large scale, the ES-175 featured a single pickup close to the fingerboard. Its mellow sound was popular with jazz guitarists. The ES-175 remains in production today.

Fender Stratocaster

This guitar, probably the most familiar make of electric guitar, is an enduring classic. Along with the Gibson Les Paul, the "Strat" has played a major role in the history of rock music.

Fender Telecaster

Under its original name – The Broadcaster – the Telecaster was the first mass-produced solid-body electric guitar. The name was changed because the Gretsch company had already labeled some of their drum products "Broadkaster."

Jackson Soloist

The first of the "Superstrats." Geared toward fast rock players, the Soloist has a two-octave fingerboard and a Floyd Rose locking tremolo unit.

This instrument used elements of Gibson's hallmark arch-top body. While Gibson and Fender have produced many other solid-body models throughout the past 40 years, virtually every famous rock guitarist has at some point been associated with one of these three instruments. Despite periodic modifications, these guitars have remained in production ever since.

THE MODERN GUITAR

There have been few major developments in recent years – manufacturers have concentrated on refining classic models. This has led to the evolution of the "Superstrat" genre. These are modern, hi-tech guitars but are nonetheless based firmly on the original Fender Stratocaster.

The Japanese, who were originally known for their cheap imitations of Fender and Gibson guitars, now produce many high-quality instruments. Guitar synthesizers have slowly increased in popularity. This is largely due to the advent of MIDI. It remains to be seen if synthesizers can capture the imagination of more than a few guitarists.

THE ROCK ERA

THERE WAS A TIME when rock meant more than just music. A person's views on rock and pop were likely to say as much about them as their haircut, dress, and political views. It was the world's first youth culture, and the world was divided into two camps: there were those who "rocked," and there were those who did not. Things have inevitably changed: rock music has grown up. The Rolling Stones, the apotheosis of teenage rebellion, still perform to millions of fans even though they are all over 50 years old. Rock has become an established musical form, enjoyed by people of all ages throughout the world.

THE BIRTH OF ROCK GUITAR

It is impossible to say exactly where and when rock guitar began. There is a direct line of heritage that runs from the blues and ethnic music of the early part of the 20th century right through to the popular Rhythm and Blues bands of the 1940s. Until then its popularity was largely restricted to the black American audience. The first guitar "heroes" were blues musicians such as Muddy Waters and B. B. King. These players became noted for

playing the straight electric blues and soloing styles that, a decade later, would influence many of the early rock bands.

It was not until Rhythm and Blues evolved into Rock and Roll in the early 1950s that the music began to reach a wider audience. Chuck Berry was one of rock's pioneers – his rhythm playing and unmistakable solos influenced a generation of budding guitarists. At the same time, country musicians began to make a big

impression. Elvis Presley's guitarist, Scotty Moore, while never a household name, is considered by many to be the first true rock guitarist.

BRITISH INVASION

Rock music came of age in the 1960s. By this time, the electric guitar-based pop group was the standard ensemble. British groups such as the Beatles quickly gained massive worldwide success. During the

Jimmy Page
Led Zeppelin was formed by Jimmy Page in 1968 from the ashes of the English R&B group the Yardbirds – a band that had already spawned guitarists Eric Clapton and Jeff Beck. Page's playing continues to influence many young rock musicians.

same period the British "blues boom" brought a seemingly endless stream of virtuoso electric guitarists to prominence. Players such as Eric Clapton, Jeff Beck, and Peter Green are still revered decades later. They were among the first rock players to combine the raw emotion and energy of the great bluesmen with a more technically accomplished playing technique.

Eric Clapton
Cream, featuring the guitar playing of Eric Clapton, was one of the first heavy rock groups.

ROCK GOES HEAVY

The second half of the 1960s gave birth to Heavy Rock. The British group Cream, featuring Eric Clapton, is often cited as a pioneer. The overriding features were loud, distorted guitar riffs played in unison with the bass, and extremely fast solos. This period also saw the brief emergence of the single most significant electric guitar player in rock history – Jimi Hendrix. Although barely four years passed between his first album and his death in 1970, Hendrix redefined electric guitar playing. While his playing technique was formidable, if unorthodox, he was perhaps the first prominent guitarist to experiment with soundscapes.

Heavy Metal, a harder, faster, and louder form of rock, dominated the 1970s. While often criticized for the nature of their lyrics, bands such as Deep Purple and Led Zeppelin achieved great popularity. However, they became highly unfashionable in the late 1970s when

Joe Satriani
American Joe Satriani is one of the great virtuoso guitarists of the 1990s.

JIMI HENDRIX (1942–1970)

In a brief career, Hendrix revolutionized rock guitar playing. Initially a back-up player for US soul acts, he moved to London in 1966 to form the Jimi Hendrix Experience, with British musicians Noel Redding and Mitch Mitchell. His first three albums, "Are You Experienced?," "Axis: Bold as Love," and "Electric Ladyland," stand up as timeless classics of the genre.

Left-hander

Although left-handed, Hendrix played a right-handed Fender Stratocaster. With the volume and tone controls directly beneath his forearm, he was able to integrate them into his playing style.

the British Punk Rock explosion "outlawed" guitar solos. Punk saw a return to the raw energy of the 60s beat groups.

FRAGMENTING STYLES

During the 1980s Heavy Metal, which had managed to retain a hard core of followers, began to fragment into subcultures including Speed Thrash and Death Metal. This music was even faster, often with complex song structures and doom-laden

(if usually tongue-in-cheek) lyrics. In the early 1990s rock music became fashionable once again – the US Grunge explosion adopted a "Punk" attitude to produce a slower, but relatively traditional, form of rock. The Seattle, USA-based groups Nirvana and Pearl Jam in particular have achieved recognition throughout the world.

FUTURE DEVELOPMENTS

While rock has not developed radically in recent years, the guitar playing has evolved considerably. American players Steve Vai, Joe Satriani, and Eddie Van Halen are

probably the most progressive of their generation. Van Halen is best known for popularizing the vogue for finger tapping – a technique in which both hands are used to "hammer-on" the strings, allowing solos to be executed at incredible speed. Steve Vai is also actively involved in guitar design with the Ibanez company.

Rock music itself now covers a bewildering array of often mutually exclusive subcultures, each one of them spawning its own stars, followers, fanzines, and fashions. While rock music may have long since lost the ability to be truly subversive, there are now probably more recordings of rock and pop sold throughout the world than of any other type of music.

Steve Vai
Former Frank Zappa protegé Steve Vai frequently tops polls in the most popular guitar magazines.

SOLID-BODY ELECTRIC GUITAR

WHILE ACOUSTIC and electrified acoustic guitars play a significant role in rock music, it is the solid-body electric guitar that is most widely used by rock musicians. Some of the most popular guitars – for example, the Fender Stratocaster, Fender Telecaster, and Gibson Les Paul – are variations on models designed over 40 years ago. Significant developments have been in extending the fingerboard to cover two octaves, the use of "active" circuitry to improve the range of pickups, and revising hardware such as the tremolo arm systems.

GUITAR SOUND

The variables that govern the sound of a guitar are difficult to pinpoint, although the type of wood used to make the body, neck, and fingerboard is undoubtedly the most important factor. The body is usually carved from a high-density hardwood such as ash, walnut, mahogany, or maple. The denser the materials, the better the "sustain" – the time it takes for a note to fade away. Some makers have also experimented using a mixture of laminated woods.

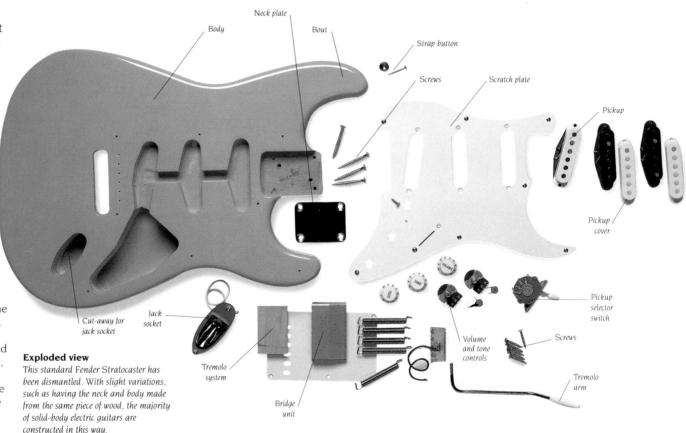

Body

Neck plate

Bout

Strap button

Screws

Scratch plate

Pickup

Pickup cover

Pickup selector switch

Volume and tone controls

Screws

Tremolo arm

Bridge unit

Tremolo system

Jack socket

Cut-away for jack socket

Exploded view
This standard Fender Stratocaster has been dismantled. With slight variations, such as having the neck and body made from the same piece of wood, the majority of solid-body electric guitars are constructed in this way.

NECK AND FINGERBOARD

The neck of the guitar is usually constructed from a separate piece of wood, which is bolted or glued on to the body. Some manufacturers, most notably Gibson, favor a "straight through" neck, in which the bridge and neck are created from a single piece of wood. The fingerboard – on which the nickel frets are placed – is usually a piece of maple, rosewood, or ebony that is glued firmly on to the front of the neck. The necks on most solid-body guitars are also fitted with a truss rod – a strip of metal that passes through the neck, giving it additional strength.

Neck features
The Stratocaster features a solid maple neck bolted onto the body. The truss rod can be adjusted at the body end of the neck.

Machine heads

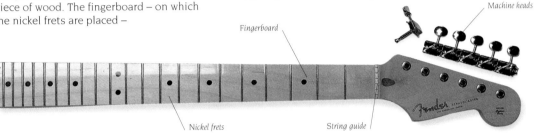
Fingerboard

Nickel frets   String guide

STRINGS

The type of strings that you use can dramatically affect the sound and playability of your guitar. Electric guitars always use steel strings, of which there are three types: roundwound, flatwound, and groundwound. Nearly all rock players use roundwound strings because they have a brighter sound, wider tonal response, and better sustain. The gauge, or thickness, of the string is also important. Lighter strings are easier to play and easier to bend, but they produce a lower volume and are harder to keep in tune.

Nickel-wound guitar strings

PICKUPS

All electric guitars are fitted with magnetic pickups which are placed directly beneath the guitar strings. They are made by winding copper wire around a series of magnets to generate a magnetic field. When a string is played it vibrates and disturbs the magnetic field; the vibration is then converted into electrical impulses, fed into an amplifier, magnified, and transformed back into soundwaves by the loudspeaker. Some pickups are made up of two separate coils. Known as "humbuckers," or twin-coil pickups, they were originally developed to reduce interference, but they also produce a fatter, if less biting, treble sound favored

Twin-coil pickup

Single-coil pickup

by many rock guitarists. Most electric guitars have at least two pickups – one near the bridge that produces a bright, crisp tone, and another that is placed near the fingerboard and produces a more mellow sound.

Nut clamp
The strings are wound on and tuned in the usual way at the machine heads. Each string is then clamped at the nut using an allen key.

Bridge adjustment
The strings are clamped behind the bridge. Each string has its own fine-tuning adjustment screw. The major disadvantage in this system is that changing strings is time-consuming.

TREMOLO SYSTEMS

The tremolo arm is a mechanical device that rocks the bridge, altering the tension and pitch of the strings. Tremolo units have been fitted to guitars since the 1950s, when their unique "twang" effect became a hallmark sound for players such as Duane Eddy, Hank Marvin, and Dick Dale. Some guitarists saw the potential for dramatic alterations in pitch, which often resulted in the guitar being rendered out of tune when the arm was returned to its neutral position. The solution was the locking tremolo system developed by guitarist Floyd Rose. His system has been so successful that alternative tremolo units are now rarely used.

THE BASICS

THIS BOOK USES a variety of methods to teach the fundamentals of rock guitar. Exercises are shown using standard music notation (five-line staves), guitar tablature, and visual diagrams. You can also listen to examples played on the accompanying compact disc. *Play Rock Guitar* gives you the option of learning any way you choose. If you decide that you want to learn how to sight-read, you can. Conversely, if you want to learn a few chord shapes and are less concerned with whole notes, augmented chords, and pentatonic scales, that's also fine.

THE NOTES

The guitar uses 12 different notes, the same as those on a piano keyboard. The interval between each note is called a "half step." The white notes are named from A to G. The black notes are "enharmonic" – they can have two possible names. They may be named after the note to their immediate left, in which case they are "sharp" and shown followed by a ♯ symbol. They can also be named after the note to the immediate right, in which case they are "flat" and shown with a ♭ symbol. These letters are repeated continually along the keyboard. The interval between every 12 notes – where the note name repeats – is called an "octave."

Piano keyboard
There are usually 88 notes found on the keyboard of a grand piano. After a group of 12 notes have been played, the note names are repeated.

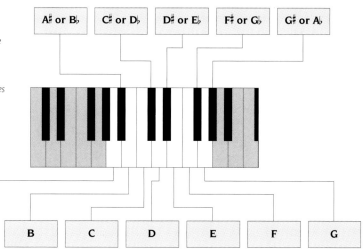

NOTES ON THE FINGERBOARD
The guitar differs fundamentally from the piano in that each piano key plays a single, unique note. With a guitar it is possible to play the same note on different strings, at different points along the fingerboard. The diagram above shows how the notes of a piano keyboard relate to those on the guitar. For example, the note E, on the open 1st string, can also be played on the 5th fret of the 2nd string, the 9th fret of the 3rd string, the 14th fret of the 4th string, the 19th fret of the 5th string, and, if you have a 24-fret fingerboard, the 24th fret of the 6th string. It is worthwhile taking the time to learn the note names.

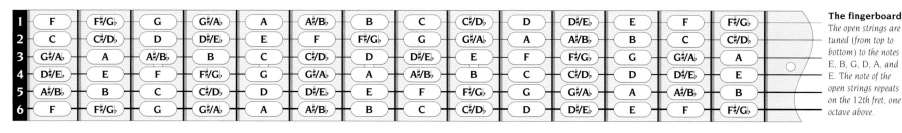

The fingerboard
The open strings are tuned (from top to bottom) to the notes E, B, G, D, A, and E. The note of the open strings repeats on the 12th fret, one octave above.

STANDARD MUSIC NOTATION

Music is traditionally written on a five-line grid called a staff (or "staves" in plural). Symbols can be placed on and between the lines to represent the pitch and duration of a note. Staves of music written for the guitar always begin with a treble clef symbol (𝄞). This defines the notes on and between each line on the staff. The notes on the lines are E, G, B, D, and F. The notes between the lines are F, A, C, and E. If a note extends beyond the range of a staff, additional "ledger" lines can be added above or below for each single note. Standard notation for a guitar is written an octave higher than the actual pitch.

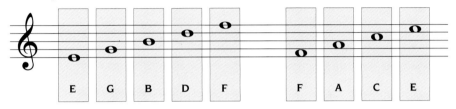

Learning the notes on the staff

*The notes appear in sequence on the staff – on reaching the note G, you return again to A. At first you may find it difficult to remember the names of the notes just by looking at their position on the staff. One way to help you to memorize them is by using memory tricks such as simple mnemonic phrases. For example, the notes on each line of the treble staff – E, G, B, D, and F – are more easily remembered by learning a phrase containing these letters, such as "**E**very **G**ood **B**oy **D**oes **F**ine." Similarly, the notes between the staff lines can be remembered as the word "**FACE**."*

TO READ OR NOT TO READ

For many aspiring rock guitarists, a major decision is whether to take the time to learn how to read music or understand music theory. This is a decision that only you can really make. It has to be said that the vast majority of rock guitarists – even some of the top session players – cannot sight-read. Greater emphasis is usually placed on the ability to improvise, or interpret a guitar part with a suitable sound. For many players it is enough to learn the names of the notes and chords, or play from chord charts (see p. 34). However, there are good arguments for learning at least some music theory. Lead guitar work is based around musical scales – specific patterns of notes – so learning and practicing scales in different keys, while not the most exciting of activities, will make you a more versatile and rounded player. It can also develop improvisational skills and help when arranging songs for a band.

GUITAR TABLATURE

A simpler written alternative is the tablature system, which is often used for the guitar and other fretted instruments, such as the lute. Tablature (or "TAB") is simply a six-line grid on which each line represents a string from top to bottom. A number written on a line is an instruction to play a specific fret.

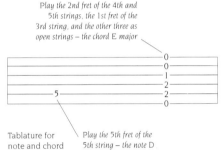

Play the 2nd fret of the 4th and 5th strings, the 1st fret of the 3rd string, and the other three as open strings – the chord E major

Tablature for note and chord

Play the 5th fret of the 5th string – the note D

TAB OR STAFF?

Standard music notation – notes placed on a staff – and guitar tablature each have their own benefits. Tablature has an advantage in that it gives the player precise fretting instructions that standard notation cannot easily provide. However, it also relies on knowing the rhythmic structure of a piece, because there are no specific instructions as to the timing of individual notes. Throughout the book, both systems are shown together where practical.

FINGERPICKING

Although not as widely used as in jazz, folk, and country styles, the classical right-hand fingerpicking technique is used by a growing number of rock musicians, especially for chord work. You may come across written music with the letters P, I, M, or A above a note. These are instructions to play with specific fingers of the right hand. P is the thumb, and I, M, and A are the 1st, 2nd, and 3rd fingers, respectively.

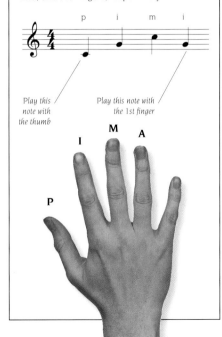

Play this note with the thumb

Play this note with the 1st finger

TUNING UP

BEFORE YOU CAN BEGIN, your guitar must be tuned correctly. The pitch of a guitar string is determined by its length, thickness, and tension. Each open string is adjusted by turning the machine head until it is in tune with the other strings. You can tune all six strings by using an electronic tuner, a keyboard, or the accompanying CD. Alternatively, tune one string and use it as a reference point for tuning the others. This is especially useful when playing in a group.

THE NOTES

The six guitar strings are tuned according to a specific series of musical intervals. The notes are, from top to bottom (or 1st string to 6th string): E, B, G, D, A, and E. The interval between top E and bottom E is two octaves. The strings can be tuned to these notes of a piano or electronic keyboard.

A | G | E

E | D | B | Middle C

LOCKING TREMOLO

If your guitar is fitted with a locking tremolo unit, the tuning process is slightly more complex. Begin by tuning the guitar in the standard way, using the machine heads to alter the string tension. When you have done this, the strings must be locked at the nut. This is usually done using an allen key. Thereafter, the strings can be finely tuned using hand-adjustable screws on the bridge.

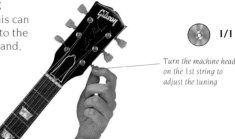

ELECTRONIC GUITAR TUNER

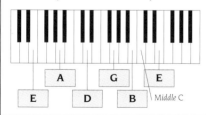

Electronic tuner

Traditionally, guitar players tuned up using a tuning fork or pitch pipes. It is more common today, especially for the gigging guitarist, to use an electronic tuner. The guitar is plugged into the tuner, and the string adjusted until it is in tune; a meter monitors the accuracy of the note. Some tuners can also be used "online," plugged in between the guitar and amplifier, so the guitar can be retuned on stage without having to disconnect it.

TUNING TO A REFERENCE TONE

1 Begin by tuning your 1st string. This can then be used as a reference point to the other strings. Play track 1/1 of the CD and, at the same time, play your 1st string (the top string). Turn the machine head for the 1st string until the notes on the guitar and on the CD ring together, at exactly the same pitch. This note is concert pitch E.

1/1

Turn the machine head on the 1st string to adjust the tuning

2 Play the 5th fret of the 2nd string, followed by E on the open 1st string. Adjust the machine head for the 2nd string until it is in tune with the 1st string. Compare this to CD track 1/2.

1/2

3 Now play the 4th fret of the 3rd string, followed by the open 2nd string – the note B. Adjust the machine head that controls the 3rd string until it is in tune. Compare this to CD track 1/3.

1/3

4 Play the 5th fret of the 4th string, and then play the note G on the open 3rd string. Adjust the machine head on the 4th string until it is in tune. Compare this to CD track 1/4.

1/4

5 Play the 5th fret of the 5th string, followed by the note D on the open 4th string. Adjust the machine head on the 5th string until it is in tune. Compare this to CD track 1/5.

1/5

6 Play the 5th fret of the 6th string, followed by the note A on the open 5th string. Adjust the machine head on the 6th string until it is in tune. Compare this to CD track 1/6.

1/6

TUNING TO THE OCTAVE

Another popular tuning technique is to use intervals of 12 half steps – octaves – to compare the same notes played on different strings and in a different register.

By tuning the first string to concert pitch, the open second string can be tuned an octave below the B on the 7th fret of the 1st string. The remaining strings can be tuned as shown below.

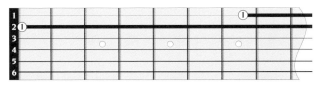

Octave B
The open 2nd string is tuned an octave below the note B on the 7th fret of the 1st string.

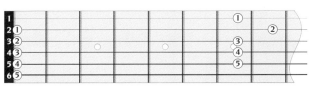

Tuning pairs
The remaining adjacent strings are tuned in pairs according to the numbers on the diagram.

USING HARMONICS

Gently place your finger directly over the 12th fret of the 1st string and sound the note. Instead of hearing the fretted note, you should hear a bell-like tone. This sound is called a "harmonic." These are commonly used in many different playing styles (see p. 45) and are also very useful when tuning the guitar. By tuning the 1st string to concert pitch E, the other strings can be tuned by matching the harmonics and open strings as shown below.

 1/7

Harmonic B
Play the harmonics on the 7th fret of the 1st string and the 5th fret of the 2nd string. Adjust the machine head on the 2nd string until it is in tune.

HOLDING THE GUITAR

I T IS EXTREMELY IMPORTANT that before you start to play, you feel comfortable holding your instrument. Most rock players are seen performing in a standing position with their guitar supported by a strap. However, many of the same players also find it more relaxing to practice or even record while seated – it can be tiring to stand during a long session. Beginners generally find it easier to sit down when they are learning.

Take care not to mute the strings at the bridge accidentally with your shirt cuff

Sitting down

Some guitars weigh very heavily on the shoulders, so it is far less tiring to play in the sitting position. Try to maintain an upright posture – slouching can result in severe back pain.

THE SITTING POSITION

There are two different approaches to playing in the sitting position. The classical method is to place the body of the guitar between the legs, resting on the left thigh. An adjustable footstool is then used to alter the height of the guitar's neck. However, this is rarely used in rock music. It is more usual simply to rest the guitar on the right thigh and support the neck with the left hand so that the neck is horizontal. This allows the player to sit in a more natural position. The body of the instrument is held in place by the inside of the right arm.

In the sitting position the neck of the guitar can be held at a horizontal angle

Standing up

Because of the informal nature of rock education – the majority of players have taught themselves – there is wide variation in the way rock guitarists hold their instruments. Some guidelines are shown here, but the best advice is to play in the position that feels most natural and comfortable for you.

Additional padding prevents the strap from cutting into the shoulder

Holding the guitar at waist height with the neck tilted allows greater access to the guitar's upper register – the high notes

The design of a particular kind of guitar can cause difficulties when playing in the sitting position. Some solid-body instruments are primarily intended to be played standing and are therefore weighted differently. In these cases, it can sometimes be more effective to use a shoulder strap to give additional support.

STANDING

The standing position is the one most likely to be associated with rock guitarists. With a shoulder strap in place, the guitar hangs naturally against the player's body, leaving both arms free to move comfortably. The neck of the guitar should be held at an angle of between 30° and 45°.

The most important consideration is to adjust the strap so that it holds the guitar at the correct height – a good rule is to ensure that the bridge of the guitar hangs at about the same height as the player's waist. It is not unusual to see some rock musicians with their guitars held a good deal lower than the standard position. While this may look "cooler," it is not a good idea when learning – if the guitar neck is held too far away from the body, the angle of the left hand has to become more pronounced. This can cause undue muscle strain on the left wrist, which may very quickly become painful.

CLASSICAL LEFT-HAND POSITION

The fingers of the left hand are used to hold the strings down against the frets on the fingerboard. This is how specific notes are played. The classical left-hand technique, which is used by some rock guitarists, has the thumb held against the back of the neck at all times. This allows the neck to be clasped firmly, providing additional pressure when fretting notes along the fingerboard.

ALTERNATE LEFT-HAND POSITION

There are many rock players, probably a majority, in fact, who can be seen sliding the left-hand thumb around the neck to rest on the edge of the fingerboard. This is an easy habit to acquire when learning. However, it is not necessarily a bad thing – it can allow the thumb to fret notes on the 5th and 6th strings, which can be useful when playing certain chords. Reliance on this method can, however, restrict potential left-hand agility around the fingerboard.

FRETTING A NOTE

When playing a note, the tip of the finger should fall immediately behind the fret. If you hold it too far back the string is likely to buzz against the fret; if it is too close to the fret, however, the string will be muted. A common problem for novice guitarists is accidentally muting the other strings. This can be avoided by keeping the fingers in as vertical a position as possible.

Classical position from behind

The thumb is held firmly against the center of the neck

Classical position from the side

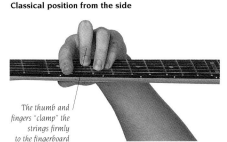

The thumb and fingers "clamp" the strings firmly to the fingerboard

Alternate position from behind

Though criticized in classical style, resting the thumb on the edge of the fingerboard is common among rock players

Alternate position from above

Some players use the thumb to fret notes on the 5th and 6th strings

Finger clearance in the classical position

Unused fingers should be held clear of the fretted note

Finger clearance in the alternate position

To avoid muting other strings, keep the fretting fingers vertical

LEFT-HANDED PLAYERS

The left-handed playing positions are mirror images of those shown for the right-handed guitarist. Many well-known guitars are widely available as left-handed models, although some players choose simply to restring a right-handed model and play it upside-down. If you use a right-handed electric guitar, you may find that your left arm brushes against the volume and tone controls or the tremolo arm. Although Jimi Hendrix found that he was able to use these problems to his advantage (see p. 7), you may need to modify your left-arm position to prevent unintentional playing effects.

FINGERNAILS

Fretting a note correctly will be made more difficult if the fingernails of the left hand are too long. A good test is to straighten your fingers and bring them down on to a horizontal surface. If any of the nails reach the surface before the pad of the finger, the nails probably need cutting. Fingerpicking guitarists often keep the nails of their right hand long enough to use them to strike the strings.

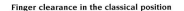

This is the correct left-hand fingernail length

RIGHT-HAND TECHNIQUE

T HE MAJORITY of rock guitar players use a pick – a triangular piece of plastic or tortoiseshell held between the first finger and the thumb of the right hand – to strike the strings. This is in contrast to classical players, who pluck the strings with the thumb and fingers. It would be difficult or impossible to play many fast solos on steel strings without using a pick. There are some rock players, however, who do find it preferable to use classical fingerpicking for some techniques, such as playing chords.

HOLDING A PICK

The pick should be held sufficiently tightly between the thumb and first finger so that it does not move when it hits the string. Take care that the remaining fingers do not accidentally dampen the strings – whether you curl them towards or away from your hand is a matter of personal preference. Most players strike the string between 3 and 4 in (80 and 100 mm) away from the bridge. Depending on your guitar and pickup configuration, you will notice a wide tonal variation if you start to play the string near the bridge and gradually move along the string until you reach the fingerboard.

Holding the pick
Hold the pick between the pad of the thumb and the side of the top joint of the 1st finger.

Pick grip
Your grip should be relaxed, but sufficiently tight to prevent the pick from moving.

UPSTROKES AND DOWNSTROKES

There are three different ways to play with a pick – using downstrokes (indicated by the "⊓" symbol), using upstrokes (indicated by the "V" symbol), or alternating the two techniques. The downstroke is made by placing the pick above the string and pushing down; the upstroke has the pick below the string, pulling upwards. Play the open-string sequence on the right following the stroking directions.

PLAYING ACROSS THE STRINGS

Each of the three pick techniques has its own benefits and can be used to create different sound effects. For example, the downstroke is commonly used to create a "chugging" rock effect. However, you will find it difficult to play even the simplest single-note solos without mastering alternate pick strokes. The following two exercises will help you get used to picking across the six strings using different stroking directions. Begin by playing the examples using all upstrokes, and then play them using all downstrokes. When you have begun to strike notes with a degree of fluidity, play the examples again, this time following the stroking instructions. Try to keep the speed at which you play and the strength with which you hit the strings consistent. If you continually repeat the picking exercises, you will probably be able to hear that you are, in fact, playing a very simple bass line.

TYPES OF PICK

Picks have been produced in many different shapes, sizes, and materials. The thickness of the pick can affect the tone of your guitar. The type of pick to use is largely a matter of personal taste: rock soloists tend to favor a small, heavy-gauge pick, whereas a thinner, more flexible pick is better suited for strumming an acoustic guitar.

Some finger-style players prefer to use picks that clip on to the fingers to create the effect of long, tough fingernails.

Pick materials
Picks are usually made from different types of plastic. However, other materials such as rubber or even stone have also been used. Shown here is a variety of widely used plastic picks.

Exercise 1 2/1

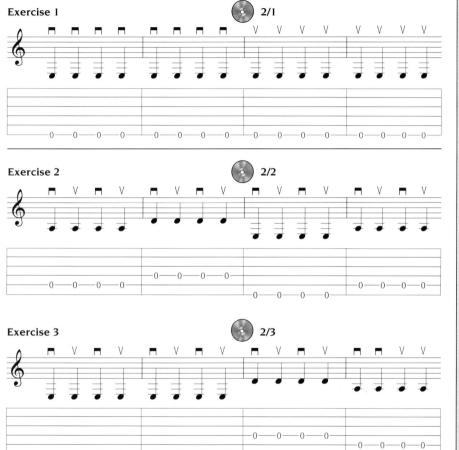

Exercise 2 2/2

Exercise 3 2/3

FINGERPICKING

Rock players rarely use classical fingerpicking except when playing chords. Here, the notes of a chord may be plucked in unison or played one after the other in what is called an "arpeggio." The classical method uses the Spanish names of the fingers. The thumb is **P** (*pulgar*), the first finger is **I** (*indicio*), the second finger is **M** (*medio*), and the third finger is **A** (*anular*). In the exercises below, **P** plays the 6th and 5th strings, and **I**, **M**, and **A** play the 3rd, 2nd, and 1st strings, respectively.

Correct wrist angle   Correct hand position

Exercise 4 2/4

Exercise 5 2/5

FIRST CHORDS

A CHORD IS THE EFFECT of three or more notes being played at the same time. It is formed on the guitar by pressing the fingers of the left hand down on to specific fret positions. You will quickly become familiar with the basic shapes and understand how they sound in relation to one another.

FORMING E MAJOR

The easiest chords to learn to begin with are known as "open-string" chords. These chords are formed with a combination of open, or unfretted, strings and the first two or three frets along the fingerboard. The E major chord is particularly significant in rock music, as the basic shape can be moved along the fingerboard to create a full range of alternative chords.

Chord diagrams
The chord diagrams provide a photograph, finger diagram, note names, notes on the staff, and guitar tablature.

E Major

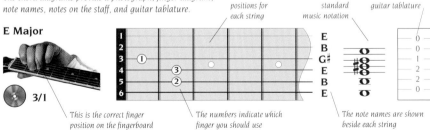

3/1

This is the correct finger position on the fingerboard

The numbers indicate which finger you should use

The fingerboard shows finger positions for each string

The notes are shown here in standard music notation

Here the notes are shown in guitar tablature

The note names are shown beside each string

PLAYING E MAJOR
1. Place your 2nd finger on the 2nd fret of the 5th string.
2. Place your 3rd finger on the 2nd fret of the 4th string.
3. Place your index finger on the 1st fret of the 3rd string.
4. Now play across all six strings.

A MAJOR AND D MAJOR
On the right you will find diagrams for another two chords: A major and D major. When you play the A major chord, the 6th string is optional – the note is shown alongside the chord diagram in brackets.

Similarly, when playing D major, some people use only the top four strings, even though the note A on the 5th string is a part of the D major chord. Some players also wrap their thumb around the neck to play F♯ on the 2nd fret of the 6th string.

A major

3/2

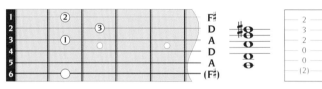

D major

3/3

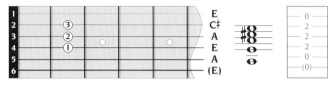

CHANGING CHORDS
The chords you have just learned are related in such a way that you will already be able to play many well-known songs. These exercises will help you to get used to the idea of changing chords. At this stage you should concentrate simply on fretting the notes correctly, and not worry about keeping time.

Exercise 1   **3/4**

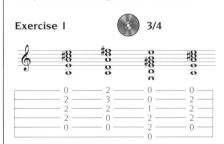

Exercise 2   **3/5**

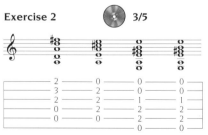

BASIC OPEN-STRING CHORDS

Here are some more chords. You will notice that there are some "minor" chords. This is the effect of "flatting" one of the notes of a major chord (see p. 28). Alternate E major and E minor chords to hear the effect. Strings that should not be played are marked with a cross (**X**).

G major

3/6

G
B
G
D
B
G

3	
(3)	
0	
0	
2	
3	

C major

3/7

E
C
G
E
C
(G)

0	
1	
0	
2	
3	
(3)	

F major

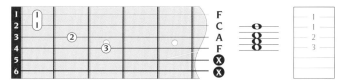

3/8

F
C
A
F
X
X

1	
1	
2	
3	

E minor

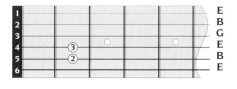

3/9

E
B
G
E
B
E

0	
0	
0	
2	
2	
0	

D minor

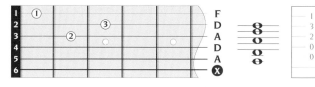

3/10

F
D
A
D
A
X

1	
3	
2	
0	
0	

A minor

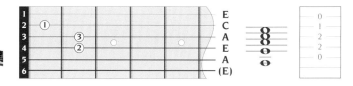

3/11

E
C
A
E
A
(E)

0	
1	
2	
2	
0	

CHORD FLUENCY

The following two exercises are similar to those on the last page. You will probably find them more difficult because they integrate new chords, some of which are more demanding. Try to play them as smoothly as possible.

```
0      0      0      3
1      1      0      0
0      2      0      0
2      2      2      0
3      0      2      2
       0            3
```

Exercise 3

 3/12

```
2      3      0      0
3      0      0      2
2      0      0      2
0      0      2      2
0      2      2      0
       3      0
```

Exercise 4

3/13

UNDERSTANDING RHYTHM

T HE RHYTHM GUITAR IS ONE of the most crucial elements in rock music. At its most basic it provides a simple harmonic framework – the chords – for a song. The most vital ingredient of rhythm guitar is being able to play in time. For many beginners this is one of the hardest skills to master. In order to play a note or chord at the correct moment, your right hand must anticipate the exact instant that the pick will strike the string. Eventually, this will become second nature, so do not be discouraged at first if your playing sounds ragged or inconsistent.

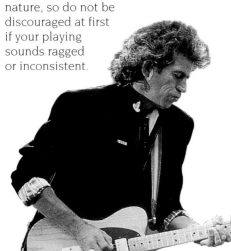

STRUMMING CHORDS

The most commonly used rhythm technique is strumming – striking the strings of a chord in one sweeping movement. This can be done with a pick or with the nails of the right hand. Begin with the E major chord shape shown on page 18. Keep count in seconds from one to four, emphasizing "one." If you have a metronome, this will be easier.

Keith Richards
The Rolling Stones' Keith Richards is one of the best known rhythm players in rock music. By no means a virtuoso guitarist, his influential rhythm style is nonetheless immediately recognizable.

SUSTAINING A CHORD

Begin by strumming down across all six strings of the E major chord every time you count "one." A chord or note that sustains for four beats is called a whole note. Each grouping of four beats in this context is a "bar" with a time signature of "four-four" (4/4), or "four-four time." The time signature of a piece of music is denoted by the two numbers at the start of the piece. Another commonly used time signature is

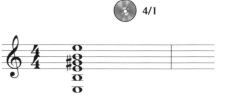
4/1

"three-four" – three beats in a bar, which is sometimes called "waltz time."

PLAYING HALF NOTES

In this example, twice as many chords as above are fitted into the same bar. A note or chord like this, which sustains for two beats, is called a half note. Continue to count from one to four, but this time play the E major chord every time you count "one" and "three" – the first and third beats. Each chord should be sustained for two beats. Play the first chord as a downstroke, and the second chord as an upstroke.

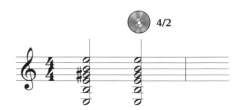
4/2

Notice how the sound changes between an upstroke and a downstroke.

PLAYING ON THE BEAT

This example again doubles up the number of chords you play. A note or chord that sustains only for one beat in a bar is referred to as a quarter note. Continue to count from one to four. This time play the chord on every number that you count. Each chord sustains for a whole beat. Play only downstrokes to begin with, and then alternate between downstrokes and upstrokes. It is quite rare (not to mention

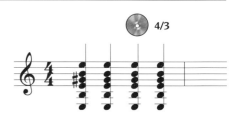
4/3

difficult) for such a sequence to be played using only upstrokes from the pick.

SPLITTING THE BEAT

A note or chord that sustains for half a beat is called an eighth note. Splitting the beat in this way creates one of the most commonly heard rhythms in rock music. In this exercise you play two alternating strokes of equal time for every beat. You might find this easier to begin with by counting "and" between each number. Smaller divisions are also possible – a 16th of a bar is a sixteenth note, and a 32nd of a bar is a thirty-second note. The smallest

 4/4

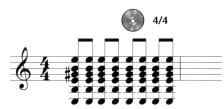

division is a sixty-fourth note – this is never used in guitar music.

PICKING THE NOTES OF A CHORD

A popular alternative to strumming entire chords is to pick out the individual notes that make up the chord. This technique is known as "arpeggiating." There are many different arpeggio patterns that you can play. The three following exercises use arpeggios based on an A major chord. Repeat each bar of music at least four times using alternating pick strokes.

Exercise 2 4/6

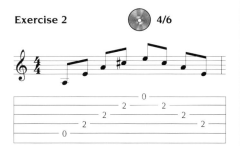

Exercise 1 4/5

Exercise 3 4/7

BACKING TRACK 1

The first backing track uses the chords E major, A major, and D major, and repeats a 16-bar cycle continuously. As with all the backing tracks, a full-length version can be heard further along on the CD: in this case, track 26/1. Here is the sequence of chords.

4/8

Chord charts
Here is a simple chord chart. It shows that the first bar uses the chord E major, the second A major, and so on. However, it gives no instruction to play the chords in a specific way – this is left to the musician to decide.

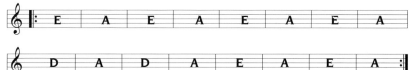

TECHNIQUES TO PRACTICE

You can play all the exercises shown on this page over the track. Try out the following techniques, changing after each 16-bar cycle:

- Strumming whole note chords
- Strumming half note chords
- Strumming quarter note chords
- Strumming eighth note chords
- Strumming sixteenth note chords
- Arpeggios

Try also to alternate the pick direction – you will notice the different sounds produced between playing eighth notes using all downstrokes and alternating strokes. To keep your place in the song, count the bar numbers in your head as you are playing – each cycle lasts for 16 bars. If you get lost, you will hear a drum "fill," which is your cue to end the cycle. The symbols at the beginning and end of the 16 bars are instructions to repeat the sequence. These symbols are covered in more detail on page 37.

E major (E)

A major (A)

D major (D)

DOTS, TIES, AND RESTS

I N NOTATED MUSIC, a beat can be sustained by "dotted" or "tied" notes. A dot following a note has the effect of lengthening the note by half – for example, a half note (two beats) becomes three beats long when dotted. When a note is to be sustained across a bar line, a tie is used. In the same example, a dotted half note that crosses a bar line would be shown as a half note tied to a quarter note.

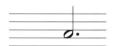

Dotted half note
A *dotted half note in a bar with a 4/4 time signature lasts for three beats.*

Ties
A quarter note tied to a half note across a bar line also lasts for three beats.

ALTERING THE RHYTHM

There is an important distinction to be made between, for example, sustaining a chord over two beats, and playing a single beat then resting for a beat. While the rhythm created is fundamentally the same, the impact can create a very different dynamic effect. Until now the rhythms you have played have been based on sustaining each chord for the same amount of time. However, in rock music, playing on different beats, sustaining a chord across more than one beat, or emphasizing chords and notes by playing at a different volume allows you to create new rhythms.

REST VALUES

The note values shown on the previous two pages – whole note, half note, quarter note, eighth note, and sixteenth note – all have associated rests. When placed in a piece of music they instruct the player to rest for the same amount of time as the note would have lasted had it been played.

Whole note rest   Half note rest

Quarter note rest   Eighth note rest

Sixteenth note rest   Thirty-second note rest

SUSTAINS AND RESTS (Exercises 1–2)

The examples below move from A major to G major. In both cases, the chords are played on the same beat. In the first example each chord sustains until the next one is played. In the second example the chords have the same time values but are punctuated by rests. In practice, rests are not generally used in this way – notes are more likely to be "tied." Here they are used to illustrate the distinction between sustaining a note and resting.

 **5/1**

 **5/2**

CHORD TIES (Exercises 3–4)

These two examples show the dramatic effect that can be created by pulling the chord change that would have taken place on the first beat of the second bar into the previous bar. In the second example, the change from A major to G major is made on the final quarter note of the bar.

 5/3

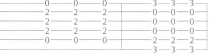

 5/4

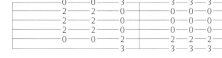

OTHER RHYTHMS (Exercises 5–6)

The final two examples give further alternatives. The two bars shown below illustrate a traditional rock rhythm. Notice that the third time the A major chord is played, it is sustained for a whole beat.

 5/5

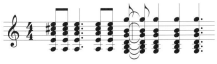

In the second example, the chords are played on the second and fourth beats of the bar only. This is a device most commonly associated with reggae and ska music. However, it is also often heard in rock rhythm guitar playing.

 5/6

BACKING TRACK 2

For further practice, play along with the second backing track, trying out some of the rhythms shown on these two pages. The piece features a different rhythm for each movement. The G-A chord change (bars 1–8, 13–16, and 21–24) uses the rhythm from Exercise 3, the C-D movement

(bars 9–12) uses the rhythm from Exercise 4, and the E-E-D-D movement (bars 17–20) uses dampened eighth notes, as shown at the bottom of the page. A full-length version of the track can be heard on CD track 27/1.

 5/8

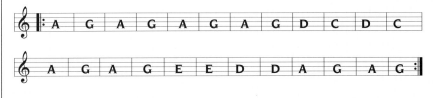

Right-hand damping
Strings are often muted by the right hand in rock music.

ACCENTING AND DAMPING

Rhythmic effects can also be created by altering the volume of chords within a bar. This can be done by striking the strings harder, or by muting them. Striking a muted string is a common rock playing technique.

There are two ways to dampen strings. You can release the tension of the fingers on the left hand as soon as the notes have been played, or you can bring the edge of your right hand down over the strings above the bridge. In this example, the first

two bars are played using left-hand damping, and the third and fourth bars have right-hand damping used throughout.

 5/7

Sharps and flats
When a note is sharped or flatted it is assumed to remain in that state only for the rest of that bar, and the symbol is not shown again. However, at the end of the bar the note returns to its original status (unless the note is tied, in which case the first pitch is sustained). If the sharp or flat is still required, it must be indicated at the start of the following bar. A note can have the sharp or flat effectively removed during a bar by the addition of a "natural" symbol (♮).

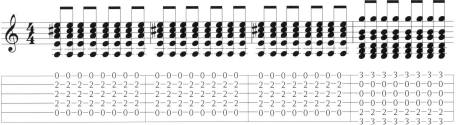

THE MAJOR SCALE

Before you go any further, you should be introduced to the concept of a "scale." A scale is a series of related notes that follows a set pattern of intervals played in sequence from a specified note to the octave of that note. The first note of the scale – the "root" note – determines the key of the scale. There are many different types of scales, but the most common is the major scale. Each type of scale has its own unique character and purpose. Other scales you will come across in this book are minor and pentatonic scales.

INTERVALS AND SCALES

A scale is defined by the types of interval found between the notes. In a major scale, the interval will be either one fret on the fingerboard (a half step) or two frets (a whole step). Learning to play scales in different ways has been the bane of many an aspiring musician's life. It can be extremely dull. However, it is crucial to have at least a rudimentary understanding of the way scales work, because scales are at the heart of all lead guitar playing. They are also a good way of bringing fluidity to your playing.

MAJOR SCALE

A major scale always uses the same set of intervals: **Step-Step-Half step-Step-Step-Step-Half step**.
In the key of C, the notes are C, D, E, F, G, A, B, and C. Each degree of the scale has a name (see above). The interval between the root and each degree can also be named (see right).

NOTE	NAME
C	Tonic
D	Supertonic
E	Mediant
F	Subdominant
G	Dominant
A	Submediant
B	Leading note
C	Tonic

PLAYING A SCALE

Try playing a C major scale using the fingering shown below. The C major scale can be played from a number of positions on the fretboard. The open-string version shown here uses only the 1st, 2nd, and 3rd fingers. However, playing further along the fingerboard will require you to use the 4th finger. You may find this difficult at first, but you should persevere. In spite of the example of jazz guitarist Django Reinhardt, who lost his 3rd and 4th fingers in an accident, you will ultimately be limited if you can use only three fingers.

6/1

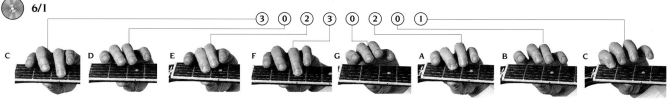

ONE FINGER PER FRET

By using the correct fingering, you should be able to play the notes of a scale without having to move your left-hand position. When playing lead guitar or scales further along the fingerboard, remember the "one-finger-per-fret" rule, where every finger on the left hand plays one of the frets across all six strings. In the first example, shown on the right, the 1st finger always plays the notes on the 2nd fret, the 2nd finger plays the 3rd fret, the 3rd finger plays the 4th fret, and the 4th finger always plays the notes on the 5th fret. You can play these patterns from any root note on the 5th or 6th string.

C major finger positions

Two alternative C major scale patterns are shown above. The first begins on the 3rd fret of the 5th string; the second on the 8th fret of the 6th string. The fingering patterns can be moved along the fingerboard to play in other keys.

When playing the C major scale in this position, always use the first finger to play the notes on the 8th fret

KEY SIGNATURES

The key in which a piece of music is played is denoted at the beginning. For ease of use, staves are shown here in the key of C, which uses no flats or sharps. A scale in F, like the one shown below, would usually be written with a flat symbol (♭) placed on the third line of the staff at the beginning of the music. This indicates that all notes on that line are B♭ rather than B. The flat symbol is not then shown beside the note.

G major   D major   A major   E major   F major

BACKING TRACK 3

The third backing track has been designed to let you practice major scales in the keys of C, F, and G. The three scales are shown on the right in their ascending and descending forms. The backing track uses a chugging rhythm guitar playing eighth note chords (the chord plays twice every beat). Begin by playing the scale sequences as shown, one note on every beat. When you are happy with this, play the scales at double speed – this means you play the notes at the same time as the chords on the backing track are being played. A more demanding option is to create patterns of notes from each scale. For example, try a sequence in C that alternates notes back and forth from the scale: C, E, D, F, E, G, F, A, G, B, A, C, B, D, C.

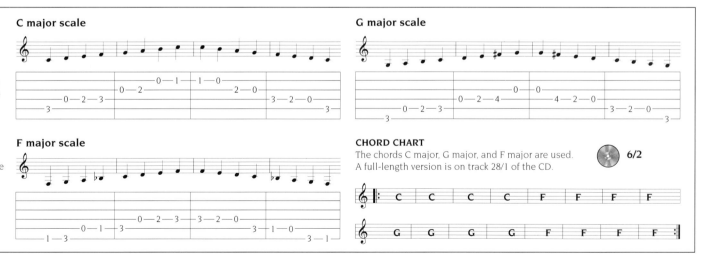

C major scale

G major scale

F major scale

CHORD CHART

The chords C major, G major, and F major are used. A full-length version is on track 28/1 of the CD.

6/2

THE MINOR SCALES

IN ADDITION TO the major scale, the other most common scale types are minor scales. The principal difference between a major scale and a minor scale is the interval between the 1st and 3rd notes. On a major scale the interval is two steps (a major third), while on a minor scale it is a step and a half step (a minor third). There are three different kinds of minor scale.

NATURAL MINOR

The most common minor scale is called a "natural minor" scale. It has the following intervals from the root: **Step-Half step-Step-Step-Half step-Step-Step**. In the key of C the notes are C, D, E♭, F, G, A♭, B♭, and C. Play the C natural minor scale shown below. The fingering is shown alongside the music.

C natural minor 7/1

MAJOR AND NATURAL MINOR SCALE RELATIONSHIPS

There is a unique relationship between the natural minor and the major scale that can make it extremely easy to work out the notes of a natural minor scale if you can play the major scale.

Each one of the twelve major scales has its own "relative" natural minor scale. This minor scale takes the sixth note of the major scale as its root, and continues to follow the same pattern of intervals from the major scale to the octave. For example, as you have already seen, the notes of the C major scale are C, D, E, F, G, A, B, and C. The relative minor scale begins from the sixth note of the C major scale (A) and uses the sequence A, B, C, D, E, F, G, and A.

If you play these two scale sequences one after the other you will hear that, although each scale uses exactly the same eight notes, the tonal characteristics of each one are very different.

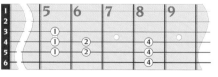

C natural minor
The C natural minor scale is played from the 6th string.

THE HARMONIC MINOR SCALE

The harmonic minor scale differs from the natural minor scale in that the seventh note is sharped, which means that the note is raised by a half step. This change creates a significant alteration to the flavor and flow of the sound.

The notes on the harmonic minor scale have the following set of intervals from the root: **Step-Half step-Step-Step-Half step-Step plus Half step-Half step**. In the key of C the notes used are C, D, E♭, F, G, A♭, B, and C.

Play the C harmonic minor scale shown on the right. The fingering requires a four-fret stretch between the 4th and 9th frets. This can be quite painful for the beginner.

THE MELODIC MINOR SCALE

The melodic minor, differs from the natural minor in that the sixth and seventh note are raised by a half step. The melodic minor scale is created using the following set of intervals from the root: **Step-Half step-Step-Step-Step-Step-Half step**. In the key of C this uses the notes C, D, E♭, F, G, A, B, and C. The scale also differs in that when playing a descending melodic minor scale, the notes of the natural minor scale are always used.

Play the C melodic minor scale both ascending and descending. Note that to play this scale the one-finger-per-fret rule must be compromised – the 1st finger must cover the notes on the 5th and 6th frets.

C harmonic minor 7/2

C melodic minor 7/3

Ascending C melodic minor

Descending C melodic minor

CONTRASTING THE SCALES

To show the differences between the major scale and the three minor scales, the following exercise contrasts each scale – this time in the key of G. You can use the same fingering patterns shown for the scales in C, but you must transpose them to G by moving from a root note on the 8th fret of the 6th string down to the 3rd fret of the 6th string. The same intervals are then used as those shown in the key of C.

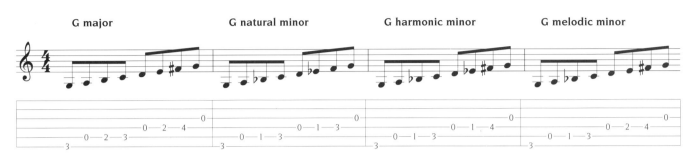

SCALE FINDER

This diagram contains the notes of the major scales and the three minor scales, in all twelve keys. Practice them so you become familiar with each one – this may not be the most enjoyment you can possibly have with a guitar, but it genuinely does pay. Learning scales will help your lead guitar playing. Many top guitarists use them as warm-up exercises to get their fingers moving prior to a performance. An extensive knowledge of scales also provides a useful framework from which you will be able to improvise more effectively.

Because scales are specific patterns, you may sometimes see unexpected note names appearing. Take, for example, the key of E♭: the natural minor flats the sixth note of the major scale. To be musically correct, a flatted C should be called C♭. However, to avoid confusion, all occurrences of C♭, B♯, F♭, and E♯ have been referred to as B, C, E, and F, respectively.

KEY	MAJOR	NATURAL MINOR	HARMONIC MINOR	MELODIC MINOR
A	A - B - C♯ - D - E - F♯ - G♯ - A	A - B - C - D - E - F - G - A	A - B - C - D - E - F - G♯ - A	A - B - C - D - E - F♯ - G♯ - A
B♭ (A♯)	B♭ - C - D - E♭ - F - G - A - B♭	B♭ - C - D♭ - E♭ - F - G♭ - A♭ - B♭	B♭ - C - D♭ - E♭ - F - G♭ - A - B♭	B♭ - C - D♭ - E♭ - F - G - A - B♭
B	B - C♯ - D♯ - E - F♯ - G♯ - A♯ - B	B - C♯ - D - E - F♯ - G - A - B	B - C♯ - D - E - F♯ - G - A♯ - B	B - C♯ - D - E - F♯ - G♯ - A♯ - B
C	C - D - E - F - G - A - B - C	C - D - E♭ - F - G - A♭ - B♭ - C	C - D - E♭ - F - G - A♭ - B - C	C - D - E♭ - F - G - A - B - C
C♯ (D♭)	C♯ - D♯ - F - F♯ - G♯ - A♯ - C - C♯	C♯ - D♯ - E - F♯ - G♯ - A - B - C♯	C♯ - D♯ - E - F♯ - G♯ - A - C - C♯	C♯ - D♯ - E - F♯ - G♯ - A♯ - C - C♯
D	D - E - F♯ - G - A - B - C♯ - D	D - E - F - G - A - B♭ - C - D	D - E - F - G - A - B♭ - C♯ - D	D - E - F - G - A - B - C♯ - D
E♭ (D♯)	E♭ - F - G - A♭ - B♭ - C - D - E♭	E♭ - F - G♭ - A♭ - B♭ - B - D♭ - E♭	E♭ - F - G♭ - A♭ - B♭ - B - D - E♭	E♭ - F - G♭ - A♭ - B♭ - C - D - E♭
E	E - F♯ - G♯ - A - B - C♯ - D♯ - E	E - F♯ - G - A - B - C - D - E	E - F♯ - G - A - B - C - D♯ - E	E - F♯ - G - A - B - C♯ - D♯ - E
F	F - G - A - B♭ - C - D - E - F	F - G - A♭ - B♭ - C - D♭ - E♭ - F	F - G - A♭ - B♭ - C - D♭ - E - F	F - G - A♭ - B♭ - C - D - E - F
F♯ (G♭)	F♯ - G♯ - A♯ - B - C♯ - D♯ - F - F♯	F♯ - G♯ - A - B - C♯ - D - E - F♯	F♯ - G♯ - A - B - C♯ - D - F - F♯	F♯ - G♯ - A - B - C♯ - D♯ - F - F♯
G	G - A - B - C - D - E - F♯ - G	G - A - B♭ - C - D - E♭ - F - G	G - A - B♭ - C - D - E♭ - F♯ - G	G - A - B♭ - C - D - E - F♯ - G
A♭ (G♯)	A♭ - B♭ - C - D♭ - E♭ - F - G - A♭	A♭ - B♭ - B - D♭ - E♭ - E - G♭ - A♭	A♭ - B♭ - B - D♭ - E♭ - E - G - A♭	A♭ - B♭ - B - D♭ - E♭ - F - G - A♭

SEVENTHS

U NTIL NOW you have used only basic major and minor chords, which are built by using the first, third, and fifth notes from the major and minor scales (see pp. 24–27). These three-note chords are known as major or minor "triads." There are two other forms of triad: "augmented," in which the fifth note is raised by a half step (sharped); and "diminished," which has the third and fifth notes lowered by a half step (flatted). By adding other related notes you can create a wide variety of alternative chords, such as "sevenths" and "ninths," which will provide you with a rich new source of musical effects.

SEVENTH CHORDS

The most common type of chord besides major and minor is the "seventh" chord. There are 10 different types of seventh chord, which are formed by adding a diminished seventh, a minor seventh, or a major seventh to a major or minor triad. On the right you will find some of the more commonly used sevenths. By using the diagram of scales (shown on p. 27), you can transpose these chords to all the other keys. To understand the terminology behind chord structures and their names, refer to the diagram below. This shows how chords can be described by the relationship of the notes in the chord to the root. An example is shown on the bottom row in the key of C. The chords on the right are also shown in the key of C.

Dominant seventh

The dominant seventh chord is usually referred to simply as a "seventh" chord. It is created by adding a minor seventh to a major triad. In the key of C, this adds the note B♭ to C, E, and G.

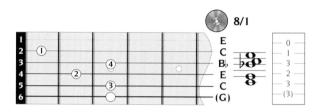

8/1

Minor seventh

Minor seventh chords are created by adding a minor seventh note to a minor triad. In the key of C this adds the note B♭ to the triad of C, E♭, and G. Minor seventh chords are usually abbreviated to "min7."

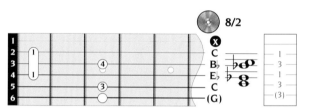

8/2

Symbol	I	ii	II	iii	III	IV	IV+ or V°	V	V+ or vi	VI or vii°	vii	VII	I
Interval number	1st	♭2nd	2nd	♭3rd	3rd	4th	#4th or ♭5th	5th	#5th or ♭6th	6th or ♭7th	♭7th	7th	1st
Interval name	Root or Unison	Minor 2nd	Major 2nd	Minor 3rd	Major 3rd	Perfect 4th	Aug 4th or Dim 5th	Perfect 5th	Aug 5th or Minor 6th	Major 6th or Dim 7th	Minor 7th	Major 7th	Octave
Degree	Tonic	Supertonic		Mediant		Subdominant	Tritone	Dominant	Submediant		Subtonic	Leading tone	Tonic
Notes in C	C	C#/D♭	D	D#/E♭	E	F	F#/G♭	G	G#/A♭	A	A#/B♭	B	C

Major sevenths

Major seventh chords are created by adding a major seventh to a major triad. C major seventh (written as Cmaj7 or CΔ) uses the notes C, E, G, and B. The E can be doubled by playing the open 1st string.

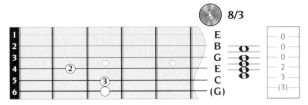

8/3

E		0
B		0
G		0
E		2
C		3
(G)		(3)

Diminished sevenths

Diminished seventh chords are usually referred to simply as "diminished" chords. They are created by adding a diminished seventh to a diminished triad. C diminished seventh is usually abbreviated to C°.

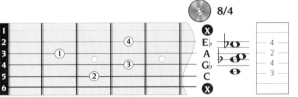

8/4

X		
E♭		4
A		2
G♭		4
C		3
X		

Seventh diminished fifths

Seventh diminished fifth chords (referred to as "seven flat fives," and usually written 7♭5 or 7-5) are created by adding a minor seventh to a diminished triad. In the key of C this uses the notes C, E♭, G♭, and B♭.

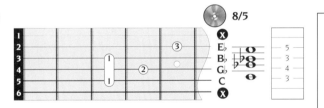

8/5

X		
E♭		5
B♭		3
G♭		4
C		3
X		

Seventh augmented fifth

Seventh augmented fifth chords (referred to as "seven sharp fives," written 7+5) are created by adding a minor seventh to an augmented triad. In the key of C it uses the notes C, E, G♯, and B♭.

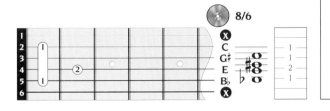

8/6

X		
C		1
G♯		1
E		2
B♭		1
X		

C minor/major seventh

Minor/major sevenths are created by combining the root, perfect fifth, major seventh, and minor third notes. The chord C major/minor seventh (written as C-Δ7) consists of the notes C, E♭, G, and B.

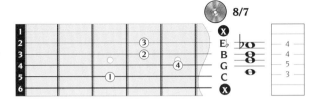

8/7

X		
E♭		4
B		4
G		5
C		3
X		

C7 half-diminished

Half-diminished seventh chords combine the root, minor 3rd, diminished fifth, and minor seventh notes. The chord C7 half-diminished (written as Cm7♭5 or Cm7-5) uses the notes C, E♭, G♭, and B♭.

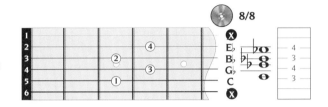

8/8

X		
E♭		4
B♭		3
G♭		4
C		3
X		

SEVENTHS EXERCISE

This exercise features some of the seventh chords shown above. The chords you need are:
- A major, A seventh, and A major seventh (AΔ)
- D major seventh (DΔ) and D minor seventh
- B diminished seventh (B°)
- E seventh

These chords can all be found in the Chord Directory (see pp. 65–75).

The first three bars show a common movement from the major chord through the major seventh to the dominant seventh. As an alternative to playing the diminished seventh in bar 7, a half-diminished seventh chord creates a more melancholy effect. You can play B half-diminished seventh by fretting the version shown above in the key of C and moving the shape down by one fret.

 8/9

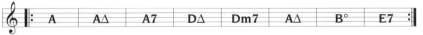

| A | AΔ | A7 | DΔ | Dm7 | AΔ | B° | E7 |

EXTENDING CHORDS

THE NAME OF A CHORD is derived from the relationship of the notes in the chord to the root. In addition to the many chords based around the "seventh" (see p. 28), there are a number of other interesting and useful chord types that can be created by adding other notes. The examples here are shown in a variety of different keys. To play these chords in the other principal keys, more detailed information, including alternative chord shapes (referred to as "inversions"), can be found in the Chord Directory (pp. 64–75).

SUSPENDED FOURTH CHORDS

The suspended fourth is created by replacing the major third in a major triad with a perfect fourth. In the key of E, this uses the notes E-A-B. Suspended chords, or "sus fours," as they are often known, are used extensively by rock guitarists, often alternated with the major chord in the same key. One of the best-known examples appears in the opening chords to the Who's "Pinball Wizard." By adding a minor seventh (which in the key of E is the note D) you can also play a "seventh suspended fourth" chord. A famous example of its use can be heard in the opening chords of "Hard Day's Night" by the Beatles.

SUSPENDED FOURTH EXERCISE

Suspended chords can be used to create a dramatic sound. They are most effective when alternated with the major chord of the same key, or as the penultimate chord in a cadence at the end of a piece of music. Try these two sequences to hear their effect. Repeat each cycle twice.

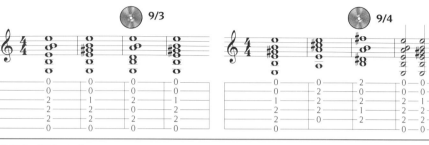

9/3   9/4

SIXTH CHORDS

There are two sixth chords – the "sixth" and the "minor sixth." They are created by adding the sixth note of the major scale to a major or minor triad. To hear how sixths can be used, play a movement that uses the chords A major, A6, and A7, followed by their minor equivalents.

E suspended fourth

Suspended fourth chords are created by replacing the major third in a major triad with a perfect fourth. E suspended fourth ("Esus4") uses the notes E, B, E, A, B, and E. All six strings can be played.

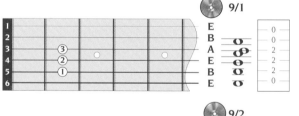

9/1

```
E   0
B   0
A   2
E   2
B   2
E   0
```

E seventh suspended fourth

Seventh suspended fourth chords are created by adding a minor seventh to a suspended fourth. In the key of E this uses the notes E, B, D, A, B, and E. All six strings can be played.

9/2

```
E   0
B   0
A   2
D   0
B   2
E   0
```

A sixth

Sixth chords are created by adding a major sixth to a major triad. The chord A sixth (usually referred to as "A6") uses the notes A, E, A, C♯, and F♯. As in most open A chords, playing the 6th string is optional.

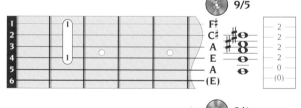

9/5

```
F♯   2
C♯   2
A    2
E    2
A    0
(E) (0)
```

A minor sixth

Minor sixth chords are created by adding a major sixth note to a minor triad. The chord A minor sixth (usually referred to as "A minor 6," and written as "Amin6") uses the notes A, E, A, C, and F♯.

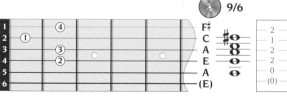

9/6

```
F♯   2
C    1
A    2
E    2
A    0
(E) (0)
```

EXTENDED CHORDS

While there are only seven different notes in a major or minor scale, whenever a note that is more than an octave from the root is added, it creates what is known as an "extended" chord. A "second" added above the octave becomes a "ninth" (it is the seven notes of the scale plus the first two notes of the extended scale). In the same way, a "fourth" becomes an "eleventh," and a "sixth" becomes a "thirteenth."

NINTHS

A ninth chord is created by adding a major second an octave above a chosen seventh chord. For example, in the key of D the ninth is created by adding E to a dominant seventh (D-F♯-A-C). A "minor ninth" has a major second added to a minor seventh. A "major ninth" has a major second added to a major seventh. Note that using certain voicings it is not always necessary to play the root note of a chord.

ELEVENTHS AND THIRTEENTHS

"Elevenths" and "thirteenths" are created using the same concept as the ninth chords. Elevenths are formed by adding a perfect fourth above the octave to a ninth chord. In the key of G, this uses the notes G-B-D-F-A-C. Thirteenths are formed by adding a major sixth above the octave to

an eleventh chord. In the key of G this uses the notes G-B-D-F-A-C-E. Since this chord uses more than six notes, it cannot be played in full on a guitar – in practice, the 3rd, 5th, and 9th notes are sometimes omitted from eleventh chords, and the 9th and 11th notes are sometimes omitted from thirteenth chords.

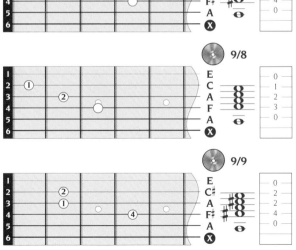

D ninth

A ninth chord (known as a "nine") in any key is created by adding the major second above the octave to a dominant seventh chord. D9 uses the notes D, F♯, A, C, and E. The 6th string should not be played.

D minor ninth

Minor ninth chords are created by adding a major second above the octave to a minor seventh chord. The D minor ninth chord (written as Dmin9) consists of the notes D, F, A, C, and E.

D major ninth

Major ninths are created by adding a major second above the octave to a major seventh chord. D major ninth (written as Dmaj9 or DΔ9) uses the notes D, F♯, A, C♯, and E. The 6th string is not played.

G eleventh

Eleventh chords are created by adding a perfect fourth to a ninth chord. This inversion of G eleventh (referred to as "G11") uses the notes G, F, A, C, and F. The 5th string should not be played.

G thirteenth

Thirteenth chords are effectively produced by adding a major sixth to an eleventh chord. This inversion of G thirteenth (referred to as "G13") consists of the notes G, F, A, B, and E. The 5th string should not be played.

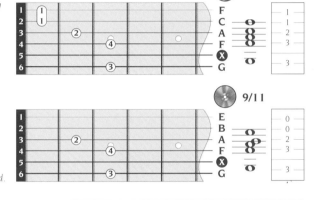

BACKING TRACK 4

This backing track makes extensive use of the suspended chords. The song consists of a repeated cycle in which sequence A is played eight times, followed by sequence B, which is

played twice. You can hear a complete version by selecting track 29/1 on the CD.

9/12

The E major chords are varied by playing the open bottom three strings which use notes from an E11 chord

Sequence A

Sequence B

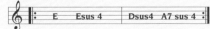

BARRE CHORDS

NEARLY ALL THE CHORDS you have used so far have been formed around the open strings of the guitar. Some of these open-string chord shapes can be used in any key by forming "barre" chords. To form a barre chord, the 1st finger of the left hand stretches across the width of the fingerboard, and the remaining three fingers are used to form the chord shape. Essentially, the first finger acts in the same way as the nut when playing open-string chords. Barre chords are widely used in rock music – without them, some of the most fundamental rock sounds are simply not possible.

FORMING A BARRE CHORD

Most people find it very difficult to play barre chords at first. This is because playing them requires you to stretch muscles in the 3rd and 4th fingers which are usually inactive. The key is to build up your strength gradually. Rest if it becomes too painful – you will be surprised at how quickly your fingers become used to it. The most common barre techniques are based around the E- and A-shape chords. However, the C and G shapes can also be adapted and played as barre chords.

THE E-SHAPE BARRE

The E-shape barre is the most commonly used type of barre chord in rock music. Begin by forming a regular E major chord, but this time use the 3rd, 4th, and 2nd fingers to fret the 5th, 4th, and 3rd strings respectively. Keep your index finger raised above the nut and clear of the strings. Hold it in this position for a few moments to allow the fingers to become accustomed to the chord shape. Now slide your whole

Preparing to barre
Practise fretting the open-string chord shape leaving the 1st finger free. Fret the chord and then release your hands repeatedly until the new fingering feels natural.

hand one fret along the fingerboard and place the index finger firmly behind the first fret. Apply extra pressure with the thumb from behind the neck. This will help the index finger remain firm. You have just turned E major into F major.

USING AN E-SHAPED BARRE

The chart below shows that by sliding the E major shape along the fingerboard it is possible to play a major chord in any of the other keys. The chord will always be in the same key as the root note played on the 6th string. For example, an E-shaped barre on the 10th fret will be in the key of D – D major.

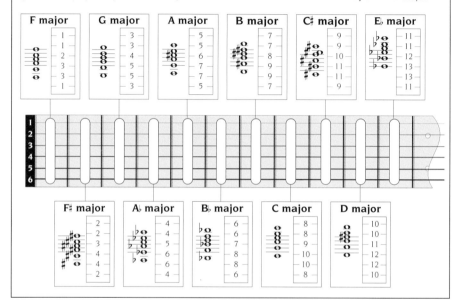

F major

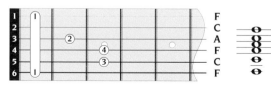

A-SHAPE BARRE

The same principle can be applied to the open-string A major chord shape. Begin by forming an open A major chord using the 2nd, 3rd, and 4th fingers. Now slide the fingers one fret along the neck and place the index finger across the first five strings. This chord is B♭ (or A♯) major.

A major

B♭ (A♯) major

G-SHAPE BARRE

It is not possible to play a complete G-shape barre chord, so the first string is not used. Form a G major chord by using the 3rd and 4th fingers to fret the 5th and 6th strings. Slide the fingers one fret along and place the index finger behind the 1st fret. This produces an A♭ (G♯) chord.

G major

A♭ (G♯) major

C-SHAPE BARRE

To form the C-shape barre, play an open C major chord with the 2nd, 3rd, and 4th fingers playing the 2nd, 4th, and 5th strings, respectively. Now slide the fingers one fret along the fingerboard and place the index finger behind the 1st fret. This produces a C♯ (D♭) chord. Using this type of barre places great pressure on the little finger.

C major

C♯ (D♭) major

ALTERNATIVE A-SHAPE BARRE

When playing an A-shape barre, many rock players find it more convenient to use the 3rd finger to barre the 2nd, 3rd, and 4th strings. This technique requires a good deal of practice as the tip of 3rd finger must be bent back at an angle so that it clears the 1st string. Some players simply choose not to play the 1st string.

Fretting an A-shape barre

ALTERNATIVE E-SHAPE BARRE

Many guitarists play barre chords by stretching the thumb around the back of the neck to fret the 6th string. This approach is frowned upon classically but nonetheless is used by many famous rock players. It effectively allows you an extra finger with which you can fret notes, but it does make it more difficult to change to other chord shapes quickly.

Fretting an E-shape barre

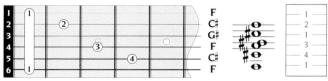

EXTENDING BARRE CHORDS

CREATING A FULL RANGE of chord types using barre techniques is vital for a versatile musical vocabulary. The concept is much the same as forming the major barre chords – you adapt the original open-string chords to be played on the 2nd, 3rd, and 4th fingers, and use the index finger as a barre. The advantages of the barre technique are self-evident. It is not, for example, possible to play a full range of chords in the key of B using open-string shapes. Using a barre you can simply think of them as open-string chords in the key of E or A, and then play them as barre chords from the 7th (E-shape) or 2nd (A-shape) frets.

BARRE CHORD CHARTS

Six alternative chord shapes are shown here using E- and A-shape barre chords in the key of A♭ (or G♯). In each case, the top chord shows the E-shape version, which is barred from the 4th fret; beneath it, the same chord can be heard as an A-shape barre from the 11th fret. While each pair of chords uses the same notes, you will be aware of how different they sound. With time, you will know instinctively which type of chord to use in any situation.

A♭ seventh (A♭)

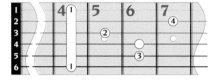

A♭ minor

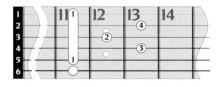

A♭ minor seventh (A♭min7)

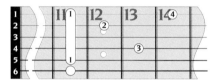

A♭ major seventh (A♭maj7 or A♭△7)

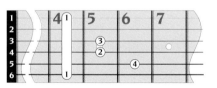

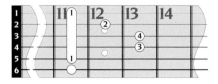

A♭ suspended fourth (A♭sus4)

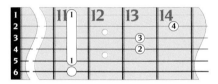

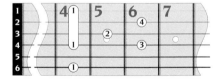

A♭ sixth (A♭6)

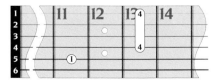

BACKING TRACK 5

This backing track allows you to practice a range of barre chords. The piece, which can be heard in full on track 30/1 of the CD, is a slow rock ballad. You will notice that the time signature is in 6/8. This means that each bar is a count of six and each eighth note gets one beat. Sequence A – the "verse" – uses the progression shown on page 29, this time with a B half-diminished seventh chord (B7-5). Sequence B is the "chorus." The track alternates two verses and a chorus. Instead of using open-string chords, play the A chords using an E-shaped barre from the 5th fret. Play all of the D chords using an A-shaped barre on the 5th fret. You may need to consult the Chord Directory (see pp. 64–75) to play some of these chords.

 10/1

Sequence A

| A | AΔ | A7 | D | Dm7 | AΔ | B7-5 | E7 |

Sequence B

| F#m | Faug | F#m7 | B7 | D | D7 | E | E aug |

BACKING TRACK 5: PLAYING HINTS

Start by lightly strumming each chord at the beginning of each bar, and gradually work towards playing chords as arpeggios, striking one note on every beat – this is how they are played on the backing track.

The first three bars of sequence B (F# major, F augmented, and F# minor seventh) may seem quite complex. Yet the chords can be played easily using an E-shaped barre on the 2nd fret. If you arpeggiate only the middle four strings, the only notes that change are on the 4th string: F# (4th fret) descends to F (3rd fret) and finally to E (2nd fret).

INTERCHANGING BARRE CHORDS

The same chords, when played in a different position and using a different barre shape, can produce a variety of effects. This is called "inversion." This exercise will help you to get used to the idea of interchanging barre chord types. Using a simple progression that alternates between E major and D major, the sequence uses all four barre shapes:

E-shape (bars 1 and 2), G-shape (bars 3 and 4), A-shape (bars 5 and 6), and C-shape (bars 7 and 8). Practice until you can change chords fluently. You can also use this type of exercise to practice extended barre chord shapes. This is a much more demanding exercise – some extensions are extremely difficult to play in some positions.

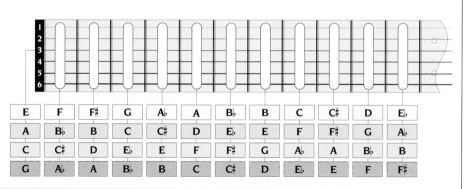 10/2

BARRE CHORD FINDER

This chart enables you to see which frets must be barred to produce chords in a specific key using the four barre shapes. Each row represents a different barre shape. They are (from top to bottom) E, A, C, and G. If, for example, you want to know where to place the barre in order to play F chords with a C-shape barre, look along the third row until you come to F – position the barre on the 5th fret. The chart is worth learning – rock music sometimes requires guitarists to be able to interchange chords with a degree of fluidity, and often at breakneck speed.

E	F	F#	G	Ab	A	Bb	B	C	C#	D	Eb
A	Bb	B	C	C#	D	Eb	E	F	F#	G	Ab
C	C#	D	Eb	E	F	F#	G	Ab	A	Bb	B
G	Ab	A	Bb	B	C	C#	D	Eb	E	F	F#

CHORD CHARTS

WHEN YOU ARE PLAYING in a rock group, unless the writer or arranger wants a part to be played in a specific way, music is rarely notated in full. It is generally easiest to work from a chord chart. This leaves the way clear for a musician to interpret the music in his or her own way – traditionally a vital ingredient in rock music.

SIMPLE CHORD CHARTS

Chord charts are often written out on manuscript paper for convenience. The basic components of a chord chart are the time signature of the piece, and a series of chord names written within the musical bars. These can be embellished with additional directions; for example, repeating a chord within a bar can be shown using a stroke (/).

In the four-bar example shown below, there are four beats in each bar. In the first bar, the C major chord is played on the first beat of the bar, and lasts for four beats (whole note). The way in which C major is played (barred or open-string) is entirely up to the guitarist. In the second bar, C and G chords are played on the first and third beats of the bar – each chord lasts for two beats (half notes). In the third bar, C is played on the first and third beats. In the fourth bar, chords are played on every beat (quarters). C is played on the first beat, and G played on the remaining three beats.

Remember that this is an informal short-hand system, so there are no strict rules. You may find that the songwriter presents a single chord per bar simply to give the overall song structure – the musicians can then do as they please within the confines of that structure.

REPEATING BARS

It is also possible to signify many other types of repeat instruction. One of the most commonly found techniques is to use the bar repeat symbol (✗) used in standard music notation. This is quite simply an instruction to play the previous bar again. In the examples shown below, the stroke is used as an indication of the rhythm –

implying that a chord is to be played on every beat of the bar. Similarly, a chord name followed by seven strokes indicates that a bar of eighth notes should be played.

There are two examples shown below. Both staves, in fact, contain identical instructions – although the bottom line is much simpler and quicker to write down and follow while playing.

WRITING A REST

Standard rests can also be incorporated effectively in chord charts. You can remind yourself of the standard rest symbols, and their time values, on page 22.

In the four-bar example shown below, you can see how sustained chords and rests can be easily differentiated. In the

first bar, nothing at all is played. In the second bar, a C major chord is played on the first beat and sustained until the third beat, where there is a two-beat rest. In the third bar, the chord sustains for three beats. In the fourth bar, the chords are played, in a reggae or ska style, on the second and fourth beats.

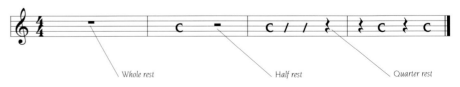

C is sustained for four beats
Chord repeat symbol
G is played on the remaining three beats

The piece is in 4/4 time
C is played on the first beat, G on the third beat.
C is played on the first and third beats
C is played on the first beat

Whole rest
Half rest
Quarter rest

NOTATING A SONG

Using the techniques shown on the previous page, it would be possible to notate a complete piece of music with ease. However, as most rock and pop songs are made up from a simple and consistent structure, the notation can be made even more brief. Here is a typical rock or pop song structure – most structures are a variation on this:

- Introduction (usually instrumental)
- Verse (words and music)
- Chorus (different words and music)
- Verse (same music as 1st verse)
- Chorus (same as 1st chorus)
- Bridge (usually instrumental)
- Verse (same music as 1st verse)
- Chorus (same as 1st chorus)
- Ending (usually instrumental)

As you can see, there are, in fact, only five different sections to play. If notated in full, you would probably have to write out at least 80 bars of music. Using standard repeat signs, the same song could be notated in under 40 bars. An example is shown above, using the most commonly found repeat symbols.

As a simple alternative, some people prefer to produce a brief chord charts for each of the above segments, and then letter each one to provide an overall structure. In the example above, introduction (A), verse (B), chorus (C), bridge (D), ending (E) can then be written out as: A, B, C, B, C, D, B, C, E.

FOLLOWING REPEAT SIGNS

This song begins with a single bar of introduction (A) – play a B seventh chord. Now play through the first verse and chorus section (B and C) from bars 2 to 17. When you reach the repeat sign at the end of the "first ending," you return to the repeat sign at the beginning of bar 2. This time, play through the verse and chorus to bar 16, skipping bar 17, and continuing on through the "bridge " bars (18 to 25). When you reach D.S. *al coda* return to 𝄋 at the beginning of bar 2. Now play through until you reach ⊕ at the end of bar 17. The instruction "*al coda*" written above the bar tells you to go to the "coda" section, which starts on bar 26. This is the ending, which continues to bar 33, where you stop.

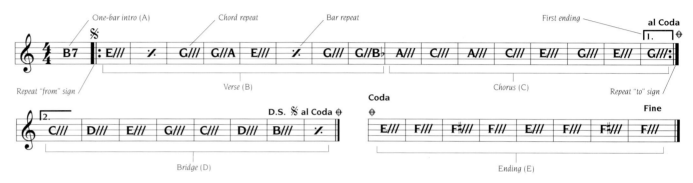

USING SCALE-TONE CHORDS

Songs can also be notated using Roman numerals ascribed to the chords on a major scale (see p. 30). The Roman numerals from 1 (**I**) to 7 (**VII**) represent each chord constructed on the major scale. For example, the chords in C major are:

I – C major   **V** – G major

II – D minor   **VI** – A minor

III – E minor   **VII** – B diminished

IV – F major   **I** – C major

Using this approach, songs can be notated in shorthand using a key signature and the relevant Roman numerals. This has the advantage that if you learn these "scale-tone" chord progressions in other keys it becomes an extremely straightforward task to "transpose" the music, or play it in a different key. This can be very useful in a group if, for example, the vocalist is not happy singing a song in a particular key. The example below shows a **I-IV-V** progression in C major that uses the chords C, F, and G. This sequence can be transposed to G major using the chords G, C, and D, or F major using the chords F, B♭, and C.

	I	**I**	**I**	**I**	**IV**	**IV**	**I**	**I**	**V**	**IV**	**I**	**V**
C major	C	C	C	C	F	F	C	C	G	F	C	G
G major	G	G	G	G	C	C	G	G	D	C	G	D
F major	F	F	F	F	B♭	B♭	F	F	C	B♭	F	C

THE BLUES

WITHOUT BLUES MUSIC, rock would not exist in any recognizable form. The blues evolved from the various types of African folk music that arrived in the southern states of the US during the 18th century, with the slave trade. Its major developments took place in the black communities of the Mississippi Delta and Texas during the late 19th century. Blues is very closely tied to the early development of rock music – post-war, Chicago "Urban Blues" musicians such as Howlin' Wolf and Muddy Waters had a major impact on the young rock groups of the early 1960s. Blues underwent a major resurgence in popularity at the end of the 1980s, so that many surviving veteran blues musicians became venerated by the public. Even now, a lot of rock music remains firmly based in the blues tradition, especially lead styles that depend heavily on using the minor pentatonic scale.

John Lee Hooker
In a career spanning well over 40 years, veteran blues guitarist and singer John Lee Hooker has influenced several generations of blues artists. Hooker was almost 70 years old when his Grammy award-winning album "The Healer" was released to enormous public acclaim.

THREE CHORDS AND TWELVE BARS

While blues music comes in many different forms, the classic blues structure is extremely simple – three chords taken from the first (**I**), fourth (**IV**) and fifth (**V**) degrees of any named key (see p. 35). These chords are played with variations on a specific 12-bar structure. The examples shown here are all in the key of G major. Therefore, the chords used are G major (**I**), C major (**IV**), and D major (**V**).

The basic 12-bar format follows the chord chart shown below. There are many variations on this structure – as an alternative, the twelfth bar commonly uses a **I** chord instead of **V**.

BLUES RHYTHM

Blues can be played using a variety of different rhythms. Begin by playing a straight 4/4 blues in the key of G, giving each chord a value of an eighth note (in other words, play the chord twice each beat). Use E-shaped barre chords and downstrokes with your pick. Only the first two bars are shown – this should be enough to give a feel for the rhythm.

 11/1

```
—3-3-3-3-3-3-3-3—|—3-3-3-3-3-3-3-3—
—3-3-3-3-3-3-3-3—|—3-3-3-3-3-3-3-3—
—4-4-4-4-4-4-4-4—|—4-4-4-4-4-4-4-4—
—5-5-5-5-5-5-5-5—|—5-5-5-5-5-5-5-5—
—5-5-5-5-5-5-5-5—|—5-5-5-5-5-5-5-5—
—3-3-3-3-3-3-3-3—|—3-3-3-3-3-3-3-3—
```

BLUES BOOGIE

This is a "shuffle" or "boogie" rhythm. To get a feel for it, play the G major chord and count aloud. Stress the numbers shown in bold: **1**23**2**23**3**24**2**3. Repeat, leaving out the middle note in each beat. Your rhythm will sound as if the beat were divided in three parts (11/2, bar 2). Although it may also be written as if the beat were divided in two (11/1) or four (11/2, bar 1) parts, the sounds matching these examples are similar.

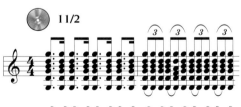 **11/2**

```
—3-3-3—3-3-3-3-3—|—3-3-3—3-3-3-3-3—
—3-3-3—3-3-3-3-3—|—3-3-3—3-3-3-3-3—
—4-4-4—4-4-4-4-4—|—4-4-4—4-4-4-4-4—
—5-5-5—5-5-5-5-5—|—5-5-5—5-5-5-5-5—
—5-5-5—5-5-5-5-5—|—5-5-5—5-5-5-5-5—
—3-3-3—3-3-3-3-3—|—3-3-3—3-3-3-3-3—
```

G major

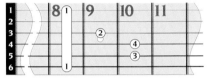

C major

D major

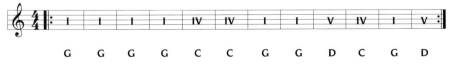

G   G   G   G   C   C   G   G   D   C   G   D

EXTENDING BLUES CHORDS

A common addition to the standard 12-bar blues structure is to incorporate other types of chord. To create a melancholy effect, blues can frequently be heard using only minor chords. The structure remains the same as that shown on the previous page, only in this case the chords used are G minor, C minor, and D minor. Another common variation is to play "sixth" and "seventh" chords (see p. 28). In fact, as a variation, seventh chords are often used to play the entire cycle, or they can be introduced as shown in the example below.

Blues using minor chords

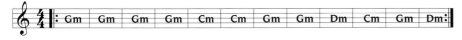

Blues using sevenths

BLUES VARIATIONS

The 12-bar repeating structures are also referred to as "blues turnarounds." Many embellishments can be made to a blues turnaround, especially when using barre chords. A popular variation can be added in the ninth bar, when the **V** chord moves back to the **IV** chord. In the example shown above (D7 to C7) the intervening C#7 chord can be introduced with great effect. Try playing the example again, only play a C#7 chord (sliding the barre shape down by one fret) on the fourth beat of the ninth bar before moving to C7 on the next beat.

6/8 RHYTHM

Sometimes you may see a boogie rhythm written out in a time signature of 6/8 or 12/8. You can work out the rhythm by saying 123456123456, and emphasizing "**1**" and, to a lesser extent, "**4**."

BACKING TRACK EXERCISE

This sequence adds sixth and seventh notes to a 12-bar cycle in G – a classic rock-and-roll sound. Although only the bottom two strings are used, it is easier to form an E-shaped barre and play the additional notes with the 4th finger. Play the sequence with backing track 6, which can be heard in full on track 31/1 of the CD.

 11/3

BASIC LEAD TECHNIQUES

PLAYING ROCK LEAD GUITAR is not simply a matter of picking out notes from an appropriate scale such as the minor pentatonic "blues scale." There are many interesting techniques, such as string-bending, sliding, and hammering, that can embellish a melody and add excitement and emotion to a performance. You will recognize many of these techniques as soon as you play them. Some of them, while a little clichéd, remain a fundamental part of rock music.

| I | STEP + HALF STEP | II | STEP | III | STEP | IV | STEP + HALF STEP | V | STEP | I |

ALTERNATIVE SCALES

You have already encountered the major and minor scales from which most popular melodies derive (see pp. 24 and 26). These are known as the "diatonic" scales. There are, however a number of other types of scale – known as "synthetic" scales – that can be created by selecting different patterns of intervals. The minor pentatonic scale, sometimes referred to as the "blues scale," has been widely used since blues and rock music first began. If you want to develop your knowledge of scales further, the modal system is also worth investigating – this is a set of seven scales that each possess a unique sound and character.

MINOR PENTATONIC SCALE

A pentatonic scale is made up of five notes. The minor pentatonic intervals are shown above. In the key of E, the notes used are E, G, A, B, D, and E. Below, you will find the fingering for an E minor pentatonic scale that uses open strings. The same pattern can be played at other positions along the fingerboard by adding the 4th finger. The example shown is in the key of A.

Open-string E minor pentatonic scale 12/1

A minor pentatonic scale on the 5th fret 12/2

ADDING NOTES TO A BLUES SCALE

Blues and rock solos are rarely played using only the notes drawn from the minor pentatonic scale. There are a number of common additions that can be made. The most frequently used addition is the flatted fifth (see p. 28 if you need to check the way that scale intervals are named); the major third is also used.

The fingering diagram shown below is for the key of E. The flatted fifth is the note B♭ – this is shown by the blue dots. The major third is the note G♯ – this is shown by the red dots. Play through the minor pentatonic scale twice, adding both sets of notes separately.

E minor pentatonic with additions 12/3

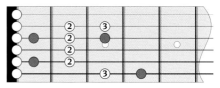

● Flatted fifth

● Major third

BACKING TRACK 7

This is a blues boogie backing track in the key of E. The chords used are E major, A major, and B major. Two alternative "licks" are shown below. Each one is shown in the key of E – to play over the A and B chords, play the same pattern from the 5th (A) and 7th (B) frets respectively. Alternatively, the patterns can move across the fingerboard and begin on the 5th string. For example, in the key of A, the pattern can start on the open 5th string and progress to the 4th fret of the 4th string. To play in the key of B from the 5th string, the pattern begins on the 2nd fret. A full-length version of this piece can be heard on track 32/1 of the CD.

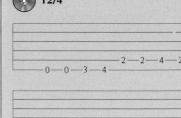 12/4

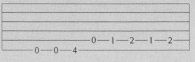

HAMMER-ON AND PULL-OFF

This lead technique is fundamental to rock guitar playing. The "hammer-on" – known as "ligado" in classical guitar music – occurs when the pitch of a ringing note is raised by moving a left-hand finger to another fret further along the fingerboard on the same string. The "pull-off" – a "descending ligado" – is the reverse of a hammer-on. You play a fretted note and release the fretting finger to sound a lower note. Hammer-ons and pull-offs can be used with single notes or chords.

PRACTICING THE TECHNIQUE

To illustrate the hammer-on technique, place your 1st finger on the 5th fret of the 1st string (A). Play the note. While it is still ringing, place your 3rd finger on the 7th fret of the 1st string (B). Let the note sustain.

To practice the pull-off on the 1st string, place the 4th finger on the 12th fret (E), and the 1st finger on the 9th fret (D♭). Play the note, and while it is still ringing quickly release the 4th finger, allowing the D♭ to sustain. Practice these exercises on each of the strings across the fingerboard.

USING CHORDS

Chords can also be hammered-on and pulled-off to great effect. One technique is to barre the three middle strings (in fact, the three middle strings of an A-shaped barre) with the index finger. A similar barre is then hammered-on with the 3rd finger, two frets along the fingerboard. In the example shown below, the barre on the 5th fret creates a C major triad. Hammering-on the barre on the 7th fret creates a D major triad. Practice hammering-on and pulling-off these chords.

HAMMERING CHORD SHAPES

The open A minor seventh chord shape, played on a barre, provides a flexible device used in all kinds of music. In the example below it can be used in a **I-IV** chord progression. Again, the 1st finger barres the 5th fret, creating a C major chord. If the minor seventh shape is added on the 2nd and 4th strings, an F major triad is created. As a contrast, repeat this exercise, but this time barre and play the 5th fret of the 5th string. Underpinning the chords with the note D now creates a movement from D11 to D minor 7. This illustrates the relationship of the major and the natural minor scales (see p. 32) – the notes in the F major scale are the same for D minor.

Fretting A

Hammering-on B

 12/5

The hammer-on is shown in tablature as notes linked by a curve marked "H"

Fretting E

Pulling-off to D♭

 12/6

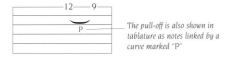

The pull-off is also shown in tablature as notes linked by a curve marked "P"

Barre on the 5th fret

Hammering the barre

The 4th finger can be used to add further notes to the triad

 12/7

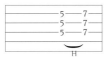

Hammering a chord shape

 12/8

Changing chords
The notes F, A, and C create an F major triad. Playing the 5th fret of the 5th string creates a new chord – D minor seventh.

BENDING AND SLIDING

ONE OF THE MOST basic techniques used by rock and pop lead guitarists is string bending – playing a note and then bending the string to raise the pitch. Originally developed by country and blues players to mimic the sound of a bottleneck guitar, string bending has become a central part of rock guitar playing. Other commonly heard sounds can also be achieved by sliding the fingers along the strings. Both of these techniques can be used to give your playing an added emotional dimension or "feel."

STRING BENDING FACTORS

There are a number of different methods that you can use to bend strings. In all cases the overriding factor that will govern the degree to which you can bend a string is the thickness of your strings. The majority of rock lead guitarists use extra-light gauge sets of strings, where the 1st string is no more than 0.10 inches thick (string gauges are always referred to in inches). Heavy-gauge or nylon strings may barely allow for a bend of a half step. For the purposes of bending, the most commonly used strings are the 1st, 2nd, and 3rd.

SINGLE-NOTE BEND

For this exercise, you simply play the 5th fret of the 2nd string with the 3rd finger. This is the note E. While the note is sustaining, push the string firmly upwards until the pitch increases by a step. You should now be playing the note F♯.

Fretting an E

Bending to F

 13/1

Hitting the note
At first you may find it difficult to hit the note accurately. If you are using ultra-light strings you might even over-bend, raising the pitch too high.

PRE-BENDING

It is also possible to bend a string to a lower note. To do this, you must bend the string *before* you strike it, and then release the tension, bringing the string back to its natural position. Place your 3rd finger on the 5th fret of the 2nd string, and push the string upwards. Holding it in position, play the note and slowly bring the string back to the normal 5th fret position.

BENDING TO A SECOND STRING

One of the most common rock clichés is to bend a note on one string up to the note on an adjacent string. In this exercise, place the 1st finger on the 5th fret of the 2nd string. Place the 3rd finger on the 7th fret of the 3rd string. Strike the 3rd string and bend the note up by a step. While the note is still ringing play the 2nd string; the notes should now be at the same pitch. This is especially effective with distortion.

Fretting a D

Bending to an E

 13/2

(7) 5

Accuracy
Pre-bending requires great skill to perform accurately because you are not able to hear the note to judge whether it is at the correct pitch before you strike the string. This is something that you will eventually find becomes an instinctive playing technique.

 **13/3**

(7) 5 5

String intervals
The interval between the 2nd and 3rd strings is smaller than the intervals between the other strings. Therefore, a single-step bend to an adjacent string from the other strings requires the note on the lower string to be three frets higher (it is two in the example on the left).

BENDING MORE THAN ONE STRING

It is also possible to bend more than one string at the same time. This is a more demanding skill. Because the strings are

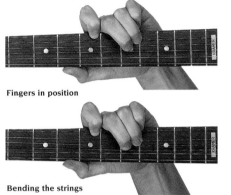

Fingers in position

Bending the strings

all of different gauges, bending strings the same distance will alter the pitch to different degrees. Once again, because of the unique interval between the 2nd and 3rd strings, bending them together is popularly used in rock playing. In this exercise, use the 2nd and 3rd fingers to bend the 2nd and 3rd strings on the 7th fret up by a half step. If you prefer, you can barre the two strings using just the 3rd finger – this technique is equally effective.

Up or down?

It is a matter of personal preference whether you bend strings downwards or upwards. It is, however, usual to bend the top two strings up, otherwise your hands can easily slip off the fingerboard.

 13/4

SLIDES

There are a number of different slide techniques used in rock guitar. The most common is simply to play a note and slide the fretting finger up or down to a different note. The final note may be newly struck. Slides can be written down in a number of ways in standard music notation.

Single-note slide

The note B is struck on the 7th fret of the the 1st string. The finger slides along the string until it reaches the 12th fret, sounding the note E.

Slide to a struck note

The note B is struck in the same way. The finger slides along the string to the 12th fret. This time, the 1st string is struck again, sounding the note E.

VIBRATO

Vibrato is an effect that can be achieved by rocking the tip of the fretting finger rapidly from side to side, or up and down. This causes a minor variation in pitch which is often used as an expressive device.

Move the finger rapidly from side to side

Vibrato technique

BACKING TRACK 8

This piece is a heavy rock track that revolves around a single riff in the key of A. The two-bar lick (musical motif) on the CD fits neatly over the main riff, giving you the opportunity to practice multiple string bending and hammering. You can play it along with the other chords by transposing the pattern on the fingerboard. A full-length version of the piece can be heard on track 33/1 of the CD.

 13/5

```
7-(8)-7--- 5----  5---- 7----          5----
7-(8)-7--- 5----  5---- 7----          5----
                  7----                5---- 7----          5----
                                            7---- 5--7--5  7-(8)-7--- 5--- 7----
                                                    5--7              7-(8)-7--- 7----
                                                                      5--7              7----
```

D.S.

𝄞 4/4 𝄆 A | A | A | A | A | A | A | A | D | C 𝄇 |¹ Em | ² Dm | 𝄋

TREMOLO ARM

Tremolo arms were originally developed to produce vibrato effects. Guitarists soon saw the potential to perform bends that would be impossible to achieve using conventional means. The first devices tended to cause tuning problems, but modern locking systems allow strings to be detuned to the point of lying slack on the fingerboard before being brought back to the correct pitch.

Operating the tremolo arm

TAPPING AND HARMONICS

Finger tapping, or "fret tapping" as it is also known, is a relatively recent playing technique. In its basic form it involves using a finger of the right hand, instead of a plectrum, to "tap" a note on the fingerboard, hold it, and "pull-off" to another note. This allows lead guitarists to play solos at an incredibly high speed. In a more advanced form, two-handed tapping, using all the fingers, and even the thumbs, can be used to play chords. Harmonics are also often integrated into lead playing, creating greater variations in sound textures.

TAPPING HISTORY

Finger tapping is commonly associated with heavy rock bands. The player generally credited as bringing the technique into the mainstream during the late 1970s is Eddie Van Halen, although another US guitarist, Harvey Mandell, was using a form of tapping a decade earlier. Jazz musician Stanley Jordan has also developed this technique, which enables him to play entire chords, melodies, and bass lines using a delicate, light touch.

RIGHT-HAND TAPPING

Here is a very simple exercise to illustrate the tapping process.

● PLACE THE 1ST FINGER on the 5th fret of the 2nd string. Pluck the string somewhere close to the 10th fret with the 1st finger of your right hand. Let the note (E) sustain.
● WITH THE LEFT HAND still in position, repeat the first step. While the note is still ringing, hammer-on the 7th fret with the 2nd finger of the left hand. You should let the note (F♯) sustain.
● REPEAT THE PREVIOUS two steps. This time, while the second note is ringing, quickly hammer-on the 10th fret with the 1st finger of your right hand. Let the note (A) sustain.
● PULL-OFF THE 10TH FRET, giving the string a slight pluck to sound the note F♯ again.

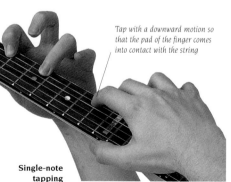

Tap with a downward motion so that the pad of the finger comes into contact with the string

Single-note tapping

SINGLE-STRING TAPPING EXERCISE

Use the technique shown in the previous example to play this tapping exercise. The same notes are used, only this time the right hand alternates between the 10th fret (A) and the 9th fret (G♯/A♭). Also, the "tap" pulls off to 5th fret. Repeat the cycle continuously. Try to avoid the temptation to increase speed while you are playing, because this can damage your timing skills – instead, decide what speed you will play the exercise and maintain that speed throughout. Tapping, while nowadays perhaps a little overused, can enable you to produce impressively fast solos.

 14/1

PLAYING ACROSS THE STRINGS

The tapping technique can also be used to play notes across the fingerboard. The following exercise is shown in the diagram below. In each case, the numbers in the circles on the fingerboard indicate which fingers you should use. The dots marked in purple are played by the left hand, and those in blue are played by the right hand. The exercise can be played from the top string downwards, or the bottom string upwards. Either way, you should play the lowest note on each string first.

 14/2

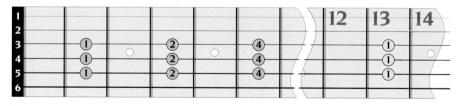

 Left hand   Right hand

HARMONICS

Harmonics are the bell-like tones obtained by playing a string when gently damping specific frets with the left hand. You have already come across them in the tuning instructions (see p. 13). They can also be used as attractive playing effects in their own right. Audible harmonics occur over most of the frets on the fingerboard, but they are most frequently used on the 5th, 7th, and 12th frets (and less commonly on the 3rd and 9th frets). The diagram below names the notes that you can produce by playing open-string harmonics on these five frets. Note that on the 12th fret the harmonics produced are one octave higher than the open string, and on the 5th fret, harmonics are two octaves higher than the open string. Play through all the harmonics on the diagram. In written notation, a harmonic is shown as a diamond rather than a dot on the staff.

FRETTED HARMONICS

Harmonics for notes other than those shown below can also be produced. To do this, you fret notes with the left hand and create the harmonic by simultaneously damping and plucking the string with the right hand. For example, place the 1st finger of the left hand on the 2nd fret of the 2nd string. Now, lightly place the index finger of your right hand over the 14th fret, and sound the note with your thumb, or with a pick held between the thumb and the 2nd finger. In this way, any octave harmonic can be produced so long as there is an interval of 12 frets between the point at which the right hand strikes the string and the fretted note.

Similarly, if you barre a G major chord on the 3rd fret and play the harmonics for each string on (from bottom to top) frets 15, 17, 17, 16, 15, and 15, you will hear the chord played as a series of harmonics.

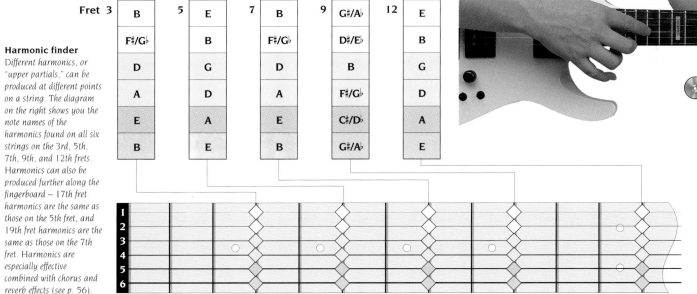

Fret 3 / **5** / **7** / **9** / **12**

Fret 3	Fret 5	Fret 7	Fret 9	Fret 12
B	E	B	G♯/A♭	E
F♯/G♭	B	F♯/G♭	D♯/E♭	B
D	G	D	B	G
A	D	A	F♯/G♭	D
E	A	E	C♯/D♭	A
B	E	B	G♯/A♭	E

Harmonic finder

Different harmonics, or "upper partials," can be produced at different points on a string. The diagram on the right shows you the note names of the harmonics found on all six strings on the 3rd, 5th, 7th, 9th, and 12th frets. Harmonics can also be produced further along the fingerboard – 17th fret harmonics are the same as those on the 5th fret, and 19th fret harmonics are the same as those on the 7th fret. Harmonics are especially effective combined with chorus and reverb effects (see p. 56).

14/3

Right-hand harmonics

By fretting the note with the left hand and using the right hand to create the harmonic effect it is possible to play any note on the fingerboard as a harmonic.

Harmonics in practice

The 12th fret is the most commonly used fret on which to play harmonics. This is because on the open strings it simply produces the same notes an octave higher. Chords of 12th-fret harmonics using the top three or four strings are often heard; they are especially effective when played over E major, E minor, A major, and A minor chords.

TIME AND SPEED

When music is written down, the two numbers that sit above and below the center line of the staff at the beginning of the piece denote the time signature. Most of the time signatures you have used so far in the book have been 4/4 time – four beats to the bar. This is quite appropriate, since the vast majority of rock music is performed this way. There are, however, several other time signatures that are worth knowing about and understanding. Most rock music is also played at a consistent speed. This need not be the case – changing the tempo or time signature during a piece of music can create subtle or dramatic changes in feel and mood.

THREE-FOUR AND SIX-EIGHT

Three-four time (music with three beats to the bar) is commonly known as "waltz time." To produce a three-four rhythm, count aloud from one to three as you play, emphasizing the first beat each time. This time signature is rarely used in rock music. However, many slow rock ballads are written in six-eight time; backing track 5 (track 30/1 on the CD) is a good example. To play a six-eight rhythm, count from one

to six, emphasizing the first beat and, to a lesser extent, the fourth. You will find that a bar played in six-eight is effectively the same as two bars in three-four. Play the bar on the right, picking out the notes on the bottom four strings of an open G major chord. Then try a **I-VI-IV-V** progression (see p. 37) in the key of G, using six-eight time; the chords you need are G major, E minor, C major, and D major. This sounds especially effective if played as arpeggios.

ASYMMETRIC TIME

Music that uses a time signature which is not divisible by two, three, or four is said to be "asymmetric." In the "progressive" rock era of the early 1970s, time signatures of "five-four" (5/4), "seven-eight" (7/8), and "eleven-eight" (11/8) often found their way into music. Although less common now, they have found favor with some of the more recent metal bands. As always, the best way to learn a new time signature is to count the rhythm out loud. Pieces played in asymmetric time are generally made up of groupings of beats within a bar which emphasize a specific rhythmic effect. For example, a 5/4 rhythm can sometimes be heard as a bar of 3/4 followed by a bar of 2/4. The two sets of examples shown on the right are in 7/8 and 5/4. Hear how the accents change from one bar to another.

Playing in sevens 15/1

Playing in fives 15/2

Playing in threes 15/3

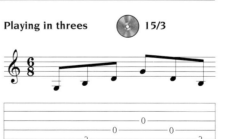

CHANGING THE TEMPO

Altering the pace at which a track is played during a piece of music can be a daunting task. It can be done in two ways. The first is where the speed actually alters – for example, a piece with a verse played at 120 bpm (beats per minute) speeds up to 140 bpm for the chorus. The second situation is where the time signature changes. Here, the beat remains at the same speed, but the number of beats in the bar changes – this can sometimes give the impression of playing at a different tempo.

When playing in a band you should look to the drummer to drive and control these effects. It is a good idea always to pay careful attention to the drummer's hi-hat rhythm – this generally plays quarter or eighth note beats. By practicing together, and linking complex passages one at a time, you will soon find that you can perform the most difficult pieces naturally.

BACKING TRACK 9

This page contains a relatively complex example, which you can play over the backing track that can be found on track 34/1 of the CD. The exercise brings together the techniques shown on the previous seven pages. It is a minor pentatonic lead part that incorporates hammering-on single notes and chords, bending, pulling-off, harmonics, and finger tapping.

The backing track is a "thrash metal" piece that begins with a riff played eight times in seven-eight time.

Sequence one is played four times. The F# chord is played on the first beat of each bar with an open 1st string E – you can do this by simply releasing the 1st finger. When the time changes, play a new chord on the first beat of each bar.

The second sequence is relatively simple. Note that on the track, chord changes are pulled back into the previous bar. Play the solo on the right over this sequence. Don't be put off by the unusual chord structure, or by the fact that the notes – especially in the line of tapping – do not seem to fit. The use of discord as a dramatic effect features heavily in this type of "death metal" thrash.

15/4

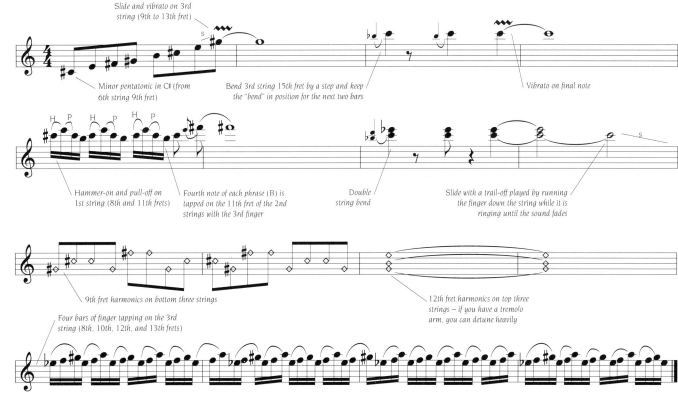

Slide and vibrato on 3rd string (9th to 13th fret)

Minor pentatonic in C# (from 6th string 9th fret)

Bend 3rd string 15th fret by a step and keep the "bend" in position for the next two bars

Vibrato on final note

Hammer-on and pull-off on 1st string (8th and 11th frets)

Fourth note of each phrase (B) is tapped on the 11th fret of the 2nd strings with the 3rd finger

Double string bend

Slide with a trail-off played by running the finger down the string while it is ringing until the sound fades

9th fret harmonics on bottom three strings

12th fret harmonics on top three strings – if you have a tremolo arm, you can detune heavily

Four bars of finger tapping on the 3rd string (8th, 10th, 12th, and 13th frets)

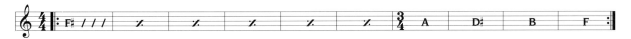

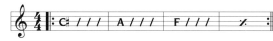

SLIDE GUITAR

S LIDE GUITAR PLAYING – sometimes referred to as "bottleneck" – developed around the Mississippi Delta, and is closely linked to the evolution of the blues. It was also strongly influenced by Hawaiian musicians. In an effort to imitate the expressiveness of the human voice, players began to experiment by sliding the neck of a glass bottle along the guitar strings. Slide playing can be used with regular guitar tuning, where it can be integrated with standard techniques to great effect. It is also extremely effective when using non-standard, or "alternate," tunings. Some slide players choose to hold the guitar flat on the lap, in the style of Hawaiian or pedal-steel guitars.

CHOOSING A SLIDE
Slides come in many shapes, sizes, and materials, so finding one that is suitable and comfortable is important. Glass slides tend to produce a more authentic sound than metal, but much depends on the mass of these materials and the type of instrument on which they are used. Slides are relatively cheap, so you should try as many different types as possible.

Nickel half-slide

Metal tube slide

Glass slide

Rickenbacker lap-steel slide

Slide types
The most commonly used slides are made from glass or metal. The type of material can have a significant impact on the sound produced.

Famous names
Many of the greatest slide players were early blues musicians, such as Robert Johnson and Elmore James. Despite being recorded over 50 years ago, a surprising number of their recordings are still available. The rock era has also produced many notable slide players, such as Duane Allman and Eric Clapton, as well as country and folk crossover artists like Ry Cooder and Leo Kottke. American blues artist Bonnie Raitt (shown left) is a respected slide guitar player. She has worked with many of the top rock and blues musicians of the last two decades.

ALTERNATIVE SLIDES
Over the years, a good many unorthodox objects have been used to play slide guitar. In addition to commonly found glass and metal slides, alternatives have included ceramic objects, bone, glasses, medicine bottles, screwdrivers, socket-wrenches, and penknives. In fact, just about anything that can be smoothly dragged across the strings of a guitar can be used as a slide. It is relatively straightforward to make your own glass slide by removing the neck from a bottle – certain types of wine bottle are especially favored for this use.

Screwdriver

Glass tumbler

WEARING THE SLIDE

The majority of slide guitarists wear the slide on the 4th finger of the left hand. Using the 4th finger makes it easier to move the slide along the fretboard, as the other fingers can be used to keep it in position. There are a number of famous exceptions, though; Bonnie Raitt prefers to use her 2nd finger, and Duane Allman used his 3rd finger.

**Slide position
from the top**

POSITIONING THE SLIDE

The most important rule to remember is that for you to be able to play in tune, you must always place the slide directly *above* the fret of the note required, not behind it, as you would when fretting the note conventionally. If the slide is not correctly positioned in this way, the note will be either flat or sharp.

**Slide position
from the side**

SLIDE TECHNIQUE

When you first attempt to play slide guitar, you should take care not to lean at an angle across the fingerboard – if you are playing chords they will not be in tune. Beginners often press the slide too hard on the strings, which produces buzz and extraneous noise. To avoid this, some guitarists raise the "action" – the height of the strings – on their instrument. This also alters the intonation of the instrument, so if you are unsure of what you are doing, leave it to a guitar technician. If slide playing becomes an important part of your style, it might be more convenient to have a guitar set up solely for slide playing.

The fingers behind the slide can be used to dampen any fret rattle as the slide travels up or down the strings. Playing slide is one area where using the classical thumb position (see p. 15) considerably improves the positioning of the left hand.

VIBRATO

It is possible to produce a vibrato effect (see p. 43) with the slide. Some players move the entire arm back and forth, while others use a slight wrist movement. Whichever way you choose, make sure that you keep your hand position steady and make the action of vibrato as even as possible. The amount of movement is up to the individual, but no more than a half step either way is recommended.

SINGLE NOTE EXERCISE

To get used to playing with a slide, begin by holding the slide above the nut. Play an open E on the first string, and slide up to the octave on the 12th fret. The directional line between the notes on the staff and tablature indicate the direction of the slide.

 16/1

To improve your intonation, this time try playing the E major scale using just the first string, as shown below.

 16/2

PLAYING ACROSS THE STRINGS

Try this E minor pentatonic scale. It starts on the 12th fret of the 6th string. Before you play the third note of the scale (A), ensure that the second note (G) has stopped ringing. You can do this by damping the 6th string with one of the free fingers.

 16/3

Repeat the above exercise in reverse, as shown below. Then repeat both sequences, playing one after the other.

 16/4

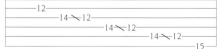

ALTERNATE TUNING

THE TECHNIQUES AND EXERCISES shown throughout this book have all used the same guitar tuning – from bottom to top, E-A-D-G-B-E. However, there are many non-standard, or "alternate," tunings that can be used on the guitar to great effect. Some of these tunings evolved from early acoustic instruments, and others originated with the Delta Blues players, who developed slide-guitar tunings and techniques along with Hawaiian musicians. Some musicians, such as Joni Mitchell, use these tuning methods exclusively. Alternate tunings can be used on acoustic as well as electric guitars, and with fingered and slide styles of playing.

ALTERNATE TUNINGS FOR PLAYING SLIDE GUITAR

The most commonly used tunings for slide playing are known as "open" tunings. Here the strings are tuned to a particular chord, and other chords can be played simply by sliding the bottleneck along the fingerboard. The four chords shown here are among the most commonly used open tunings.

Open G

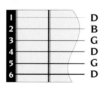

1	D
2	B
3	G
4	D
5	G
6	D

Open E

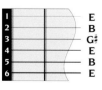

1	E
2	B
3	G#
4	E
5	B
6	E

Open D

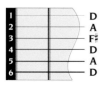

1	D
2	A
3	F#
4	D
5	A
6	D

Open A

1	E
2	C#
3	A
4	E
5	A
6	E

OPEN TUNINGS ALONG THE FINGERBOARD

This diagram shows which fret the slide (or barred finger) must be positioned above to play chords using the open E, open G, open D, and open A tunings shown below on the left. For example, all the chords shown in a purple box use open A tuning. By placing the slide above the 7th fret, you can play an E major chord; if you move it to the 10th fret you can play G major.

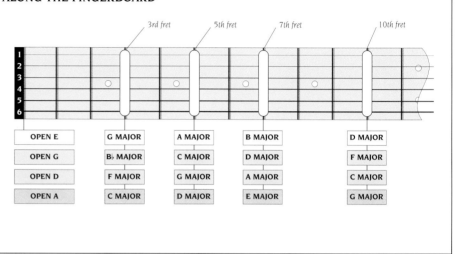

	3rd fret	5th fret	7th fret	10th fret
OPEN E	G MAJOR	A MAJOR	B MAJOR	D MAJOR
OPEN G	B♭ MAJOR	C MAJOR	D MAJOR	F MAJOR
OPEN D	F MAJOR	G MAJOR	A MAJOR	C MAJOR
OPEN A	C MAJOR	D MAJOR	E MAJOR	G MAJOR

USING OPEN G TUNING

The following exercise combines the slide techniques shown on the previous page with the open G tuning shown on the left. This shows how effectively the slide can be used in chordal work. To retune your guitar to open G from standard tuning, it is simply a matter of lowering the 1st, 5th, and 6th strings by a whole step – the two E strings change to D, and A changes to G. Play the exercise on the right, remembering to keep the slide at a right angle to the fingerboard and directly above the fret.

 17/1

Open G slide exercise
Hold the slide directly above the 5th fret and play the top four strings – this produces a C major chord. While the notes are still ringing, slide your left hand up to

the 7th fret – this produces a D major chord. With the notes still sounding, take the slide back to the original position on the 5th fret. Repeat the exercise, moving up to the 8th, 9th, and 10th frets and back.

FINGER-STYLE PLAYING

Open-string tuning can also be played finger-style, with the index finger creating a barre in place of the slide. This leaves the other fingers free to fret notes and create chord shapes. With your guitar still tuned to open G, try playing the following exercise. For it to work successfully, you should not play the 6th string.

 17/2

BACKING TRACK 10

This is a simple blues-based piece in G. Use the open G tuning and play the exercises shown on the left to accompany the track. The chords used are G major, C major, and D major. Try also simply sliding the chords from the 1st fret or 12th fret (G) to the 5th fret (C) and 7th fret (D). You can hear a full-length version of this piece on track 35/1 of the CD.

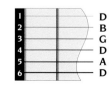 **17/3**

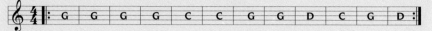

EXPERIMENTATION

A great many alternate tunings have been developed by guitarists over the years. Some have obvious uses, while others are more musically obscure. How alternate tunings fit into your own playing style is largely a matter of experimentation. It is worth devoting some attention to them. Sometimes such tunings can yield a new world of undiscovered chords to enhance your music; sometimes you may only find them useful for one song. The four diagrams below show some commonly used alternate tunings, which do not create open chords.

SOUND AND TUNING

Certain types of guitar work well with specific non-standard tunings, so it is always advisable to practice using different tunings. One musician who makes use of alternate tuning is Keith Richards of the Rolling Stones, who invariably uses open-G tuning (with the 6th string removed). He generally uses this tuning with a Fender Telecaster, producing a resonant, clear tone. Sometimes he also uses a capo – a mechanical device that fits around the fingerboard to allow open-string chords to be played easily in different keys.

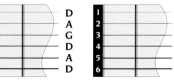
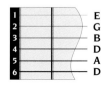

Drop D — E B G D A D

Double Drop D — D B G D A D

"DADGAD" — D A G D A D

Drop G or "G6" — E B G D G D

AMPLIFIERS AND SPEAKERS

THE COMBINATION of an amplifier and a loudspeaker is a necessity for the modern guitarist. For the majority of rock musicians, amplification and sound processing are an integral part of their art and for some it is almost as important as developing a good playing technique. Besides simply boosting the volume of the guitar, amplifiers are also capable of producing a wide variety of different sounds and effects in their own right. Choosing a suitable amplifier should be a high priority to the serious rock guitarist.

Fender Stratocaster

Classic combination
The classic Vox AC30 valve combo amplifier has been used by many of the top rock players for over 30 years. Brian May, guitarist with the group Queen, can be seen on stage using a system that features 12 Vox AC30s.

AMPLIFIER HISTORY
The first amplifiers were built in the 1930s, using the valve radio and hi-fi technology of the day. As the electric guitar gained in popularity during the 1950s, the first dedicated guitar amplifiers arrived. These models were often produced by the guitar manufacturers themselves. The classic amplifiers from the late 1950s and early 1960s, such as the Fender Twin Reverb and the Vox AC30, usually combined a valve amplifier with either one or two 12-in (30-cm) loudspeakers. These models became popular with the early blues and rock musicians because of the warmth of their

Vox AC30

tone and the way in which the sound could be distorted, although these qualities were by no means deliberate design features.

In the late 1960s guitarists in the popular heavy rock groups favored powerful amplifiers with large independent speaker cabinets, each containing four 12-in (30-cm) loudspeakers. The most famous of these is probably the "Marshall stack." During the 1970s many solid-state, "transistor" models appeared. Although this cheaper technology quickly became extremely popular, it was clear that the old-fashioned valve sound was an important part of the rock heritage.

In recent years a number of "hybrid" models have appeared, combining valve and solid-state circuitry.

Clean valve sounds
The Fender Twin Reverb is used by guitarists who favor a clean valve sound. B. B. King uses this amplifier with a Gibson ES-335. The guitar is semi-acoustic, so unwanted feedback can occur at high volumes. King overcame this problem by stuffing towels into the soundhole.

AMPLIFIER FORMATS
There are three commonly used amplifier formats: the amplifier and speaker combination, more commonly known as a "combo;" the separate amplifier and speaker; and, in recent years, the rack-mounted amplifier.

COMBO
The most commonly used format is the combo. This has the amplifier and speaker housed within the same cabinet. Classic models such as the Vox AC30, Mesa Boogie, and the Fender Twin Reverb are among the most popular combos. The major advantage of using combos is that they are portable and self-contained. However, some of the models that house more than one loudspeaker can be rather heavy to carry for long distances.

Gibson ES-335

Fender Twin Reverb

HEADS AND STACKS

The vogue for separate amplifier and loudspeakers arose with the emergence of the heavy rock groups in the middle of the 1960s. In this combination the amplifier is usually referred to as the "head," and the speakers as the "stack." Such combinations can potentially produce far greater volume than a combo, although in a small venue it can be difficult to achieve a high-quality distortion sound at a low enough volume. Separates also have the advantage that the player can add speaker cabinets of their own choice and quantity.

Marshall "Stack"
Although Jim Marshall first produced his British-made amplifiers in 1962, Marshall products are strongly identified with high-volume heavy rock and metal bands. Also shown here is an extremely rare and valuable 1959 Gibson Les Paul Standard.

Gibson Les Paul Standard

Marshall JTM 45 amplifier

Marshall 4x12 ("4 by 12") speaker cabinet

NOISE POLLUTION
Practice can be a nightmare for many rock guitarists and their neighbors. Getting a balance between playing loud enough to create a "rock" sound and yet minimizing the nuisance to those around you can be a problem. One solution is to use a practice amplifier. These are small combos – usually of less than 5 watts of power – that have the features of a standard combo. Another popular solution is to practice using headphones; many of the smaller multi-effect pedals are equipped with headphone sockets.

RACK AND MIDI SYSTEMS
Some manufacturers now produce pre-amplifiers and power amplifiers that fit into standard 19-in (48-cm) rack units. In some cases these are simply an alternative way of storing the amplifier "head." Many of the major manufacturers now produce MIDI-equipped amplifiers that allow settings to be stored, or altered from a footswitch or other external control, such as a MIDI sequencer or computer (see p. 60).

Marshall 4500 amplifier

Marshall 2100 amplifier

The "hi-tech" guitarist
This system was designed and put together by British guitarist Jim Barber. It offers complete control and flexibility, both on stage and in the studio.

USING AN AMPLIFIER

T O PRODUCE A SOUND, the guitar is plugged into the input socket of an amplifier using a screened cable with "jack plugs" at either end. Some amplifiers feature more than one input channel. This can either allow a second instrument to be plugged in, or can be used to switch between two different settings – especially useful if you play both rhythm and lead guitar. While every amplifier has its own unique set of features, there are some that are common to nearly all models: channel input level, bass, treble, and master volume.

THE AMPLIFICATION PROCESS

Guitar amplifiers work in a variety of different ways, but there are a number of stages of operation that every amplifier must be able to perform.

In a simple guitar amplifier, the process begins with an input signal from a guitar. The level and tone of this signal can be altered on the guitar itself (see p. 55). The volume of the initial signal is governed by the input channel volume control. The pre-amplifier stage boosts this signal, which is then passed through to the equalization stage. This process usually consists of a single bass and treble control, although more sophisticated models may feature a mid-range control or even a graphic equalizer. The signal is then passed to the power amplifier, the volume of which is controlled by the master volume control. This is the final control before the signal is passed to the loudspeaker. If the amplifier has more than one input channel, the master volume acts as an overall volume control for all input channels.

The more expensive, sophisticated amplifiers may have any number of intermediary stages. For example, there may be separate "lead" or "overdrive" channels, or there may be separate equalization for each channel. Some amplifiers also have built-in sound processing effects such as reverberation or tremolo (see pp. 56–59).

FINDING THE RIGHT SOUND

Achieving an appropriate guitar sound is a vital part of learning rock guitar. By gaining a thorough understanding of the way your equipment works, you should be able to combine the different components to produce any sound that you want.

Five different types of basic amplifier setting are shown here. While they will obviously sound different from one amplifier to another, the fundamental principles remain true for most models.

INPUT VOLUME   BASS   TREBLE   MASTER VOLUME

Clean sound
The controls are all set in a central position, producing a clean sound with little or no distortion. This could be used for straightforward rhythm guitar work.

 18/1

You can use the master volume control to alter the volume without changing the nature of the sound.

INPUT VOLUME   BASS   TREBLE   MASTER VOLUME

Bright treble
If you increase the treble control the guitar will produce a brighter, "clanking" sound. Boosting the treble will also increase the overall volume

 18/2

of the sound, so you may have to reduce the master volume control setting to compensate for this.

Panel controls
By altering the positions of each of the knobs on the amplifier's control panel, it is possible to produce a wide variety of different sounds and effects. The panel shown on the right has a set of controls that are common to the majority of modern amplifiers. The tone controls – bass and treble – operate in much the same way as those on a regular hi-fi system.

INPUT VOLUME   **BASS**   **TREBLE**   **MASTER VOLUME**

Input volume control
The initial volume is boosted by the pre-amplifier. Increasing this volume can create distortion.

Bass control
Increasing the bass frequencies, or "bottom," produces a deeper and thicker sound.

Treble control
Increasing the treble frequencies, or "top," produces a brighter, "tinny" sound.

Master volume control
The overall volume of the amplifier is governed by the master volume control.

▼ **7** INPUT VOLUME ▼ **5** BASS ▼ **7** TREBLE ▼ **4** MASTER VOLUME

Light distortion
*Increasing the input
volume will cause the
pre-amplifier to distort the
sound. Again, as this
boosts the overall volume
increase, you may have to*

 18/3

*reduce the master volume
to bring it down to the
desired level. This is a good
rock lead guitar setting.*

▼ **10** INPUT VOLUME ▼ **4** BASS ▼ **10** TREBLE ▼ **3** MASTER VOLUME

Crunch distortion
*With the input volume on
full, the pre-amplifier
produces the maximum
possible distortion. The
increase in treble produces
a cutting lead guitar*

 18/4

*sound. With the controls
set in this way you need to
beware of creating
unwanted feedback.*

▼ **10** INPUT VOLUME ▼ **4** BASS ▼ **3** TREBLE ▼ **5** MASTER VOLUME

Muted distortion
*Reducing the treble
produces a "muffled"
sound. This results in a
loss of volume, which is
balanced by boosting the
master volume. Some*

  18/5

*guitarists choose to create
the same effect by turning
down the tone control on
the guitar itself.*

VALVE, SOLID STATE, OR HYBRID?

Mesa Boogie valve

Most rock guitarists favor the classic valve amplifier sound. Valve amplifiers are capable of producing a warmer, smoother sound. They also produce a higher quality of distortion with increases in volume. Valves can, however, be unreliable, come loose, and need periodic replacement. They also take a few minutes to warm up. Many guitarists devote a great deal of time to experimentation, some claiming that different kinds of valves are capable of producing a wide variety of sounds.

Solid-state or transistor amplifiers tend to have a more brittle or sharp sound character. They are favored by players who prefer a more clinical sound. Because solid-state units use transistors, they are capable of producing a wider range of frequencies than valve amplifiers. They also distort less at higher volumes, which is why solid-state power amplifiers are invariably used to drive PA systems and studio monitors. Solid-state amplification is generally considered to be more reliable, and consistent from model to model, than valve amplification. However, this very fact has resulted in some players regarding them as dull, or lacking in character.

Some guitarists use hybrid systems – a valve amplifier or pre-amplifier provides the basic sound, which is then amplified using a separate solid-state power amplifier. For example, US rock giant Eddie Van Halen uses a Peavey 100-watt valve amplifier with a "load" resistor fitted across the speaker outputs to reduce the output. The signal is then passed into a pair of H+H 400-watt solid-state power amplifiers. This produces distortion-free volume at any desired level.

GUITAR CONTROL PANEL

Most electric guitars are equipped with at least a volume and tone control. Some, like the Gibson Les Paul, have a volume and tone control for each pickup. This allows the player to switch between settings easily. In practice, the majority of players rarely touch the controls, leaving them permanently "on full" and making any tonal changes on the amplifier. However, it is always worth experimenting. Heavy valve distortion, for example, can sound interesting with the treble tone on the guitar set to a minimum value. Guitar controls can also produce a variety of playing effects. Try playing a note with the volume turned off, and then quickly fade the volume up while the note still sustains.

Guitar controls
*The Gibson Les Paul has
volume and tone controls
dedicated to each pickup.
Many instruments have
only one set of controls.*

Volume for the bridge pickup

Volume for the neck pickup

Tone for the bridge pickup

Tone for the neck pickup

VOLUME PEDAL

A volume pedal can be inserted between the guitar and amplifier to provide foot control of the input signal. This can be useful when switching between playing lead and rhythm guitar.

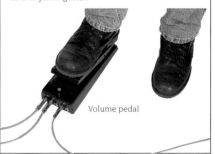

Volume pedal

ALTERING THE SOUND

B Y THE TIME A SIGNAL is heard through the loudspeaker, it has already gone through a considerable amount of processing in the amplifier itself. There are many other effects that can be added to a guitar to produce further coloration of sound. These are generally either electronic simulations of natural time-based acoustic phenomena, such as reverberation and echo, or completely artificial effects based on changes in pitch. Electronic effects can be found in the form of plug-in foot pedals or more sophisticated multiple-effect rack units. More and more rock musicians now depend on electronic effects to provide their basic sounds.

REVERBERATION

Reverberation is the effect of a sound made in a confined space bouncing off the walls a number of times before fading away. The reverberation is heard as a part of the original sound – for example, think of the sound of your own footsteps when you walk through a tunnel. When added to a basic guitar sound, reverberation – usually referred to simply as "reverb" – produces a pleasant ambient effect.

Spring reverb was the first effect to achieve widespread popularity with guitarists. Here, the reverb effect – usually built into the amplifier – is created by a small spring that is vibrated by the guitar signal. This is at the heart of the classic rock and roll or "surfing" guitar sounds, used by players such as Eddie Cochran, Duane Eddy, Dick Dale, and Hank

Marvin. Nowadays, the mechanical spring reverb units have been largely replaced by high-quality, rack-mounted, electronic digital reverberation. Such units generally have a variety of programmable parameters, based on the attributes of natural reverberation. For example, natural reverb is dependent on the size, shape, and sound-damping features of a room.

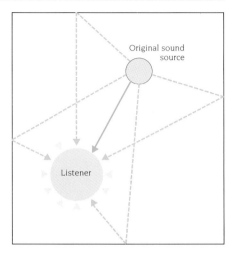

How reverb works
When you hear a sound in a room, the original source is the first to reach your ears. This is followed by early reflections from the surrounding walls and ceiling. Shortly afterwards, these sound waves are then further reflected off the same set of surfaces.

Original sound source

Listener

→ Direct sound (original sound source)

--→ Early reflection (first bounce from surfaces)

Later reflections (subsequent bounces)

USING ELECTRONIC EFFECTS

Connecting electronic processing effects to your guitar is an extremely simple matter – the units are simply inserted between the output of the guitar and the input of the amplifier. It is possible to connect a large number of effects together by "daisychaining" the output of one to the input of another. Remember that each time you want to plug in a new effect you will also need an additional connection lead. If you are daisychaining a large number of effects, it is a good idea to use small patch-bay type leads that are less than 12 in (30 cm) long – if you use full-length leads for this purpose they can easily get tangled up. The majority of standard foot pedals are battery controlled, so remember to unplug them when they are not in use. It is always wise to keep a good supply of appropriately sized batteries in your guitar case, especially if you often play live.

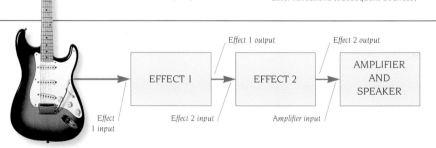

Effect 1 input

Effect 2 input

EFFECT 1 → EFFECT 2 → AMPLIFIER AND SPEAKER

Effect 1 output

Effect 2 output

Amplifier input

DELAY EFFECTS

Many of the most popular effects derive from repeating a delayed signal. This natural effect – "echo" – is produced when a sound is reflected from a distant surface. Unlike reverberation, the echo is heard distinctly after the original signal has stopped. Echo was originally produced electronically by using loops of tape that passed over multiple tape heads. It is now generally produced digitally.

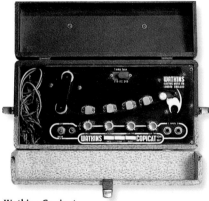

Watkins Copicat
One of the most popular guitar effects ever, some guitarists still use echo units like the Copicat for its unique sound.

A number of commonly used guitar effects are produced by generating extremely fast repeats. "Phasing" occurs when a repeated signal is heard almost immediately. This results in a subtle tonal change. As an artificial effect, it was very heavily used by the psychedelic bands of the late 1960s. When the delay is increased, to around 12 milliseconds, the repeat produces a metallic "flanging" effect.

CHORUS AND ADT

Delay effects were traditionally created by recording a signal on two tape machines, and then playing them back at the same time. The inconsistencies in speed and pitch between machines were an integral part of the overall sound. Manufacturers have tried to emulate these effects by adding pitch and modulation controls to the delayed signal. Two of these effects are "automatic double tracking" ("ADT") and "chorus." ADT adds pitch variations to a delay of up to 35 milliseconds. This can create the illusion of two separate performances. It is most commonly used on guitar and vocal sounds, as an alternative to recording the part twice on separate tracks of the tape recorder. Chorus is an extension of ADT, where a number of repeats can be modulated to create a rich and full sound. Chorus effects are also strongly favored by bass guitarists.

ALTERING THE PITCH

A relatively recent development has been the pitch shifter unit. This digital unit can delay a signal and replay it at a different pitch, allowing the guitarist to generate harmony lines automatically. Some of the more expensive units are even capable of generating multiple harmonies. The repeated signal is a heavily processed digital sample, so the sound quality can deteriorate badly. The most commonly used pitch interval is an octave above or below the original signal; perfect fifths are also highly effective.

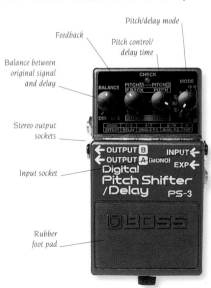

Pitch/delay mode
Feedback
Pitch control/ delay time
Balance between original signal and delay
Stereo output sockets
Input socket
Rubber foot pad

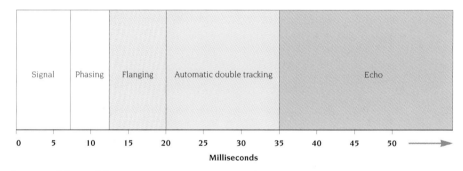

| Signal | Phasing | Flanging | Automatic double tracking | Echo |

Milliseconds

Electronic delay pedal
The versatile Boss PS-3 foot pedal is capable of producing digital echo and simple harmonizing effects. Delay effects have always been used by rock guitarists – listen to the early "Sun" recordings of Elvis Presley, and you will hear how fundamental the echo on Scotty Moore's guitar was to the rock and roll sound. In later years rock players like Jimmy Page and Brian May used long delays to build up, and play over, thick layers of sound.

Delay times
The diagram above shows the various delay effects that lead up to the production of a distinct echo, and the times within which each of the effects operates. For the first 7 milliseconds the delayed signal cannot be separated from the original signal. Phasing occurs between 7 and 12 milliseconds. This gradually progresses into a flanging effect. It is not until around 40 milliseconds that a distinct repeat is clearly perceptible.

EFFECTS IN PRACTICE

EVERY GUITARIST has his or her own favorite types of sound that are a combination of the guitar, amplifier, and sound effects. The same set of notes can be rendered completely unrecognizable by adding digital or analogue effects. To illustrate this point, several different types of effect are shown here. In each case the same guitar part is played, and you can hear the sound on the CD.

Wah-wah pedal
This unit is essentially a tone filter control that is rocked back and forth inside a foot pedal to produce the typical "wah" sound.

WAH-WAH PEDAL

 19/1

One of the most famous guitar effects is the wah-wah pedal. It can be used in many different ways. Players such as Jimi Hendrix and Eric Clapton used it in conjunction with overdrive to produce a wide array of expressive sounds. Jimi Hendrix's 1968 album "Electric Ladyland" features some of the finest wah-wah playing ever recorded. Frank Zappa often used it as an additional tone control, finding a setting he liked and leaving the pedal in that position. Guitarists in early 1970s funk bands also used the wah-wah; muting the strings and strumming a rhythm while rocking the pedal produces a sound characterized by Isaac Hayes' theme music for the film "Shaft." The CD track has two different effects: a clean wah-wah sound, and wah-wah with overdrive.

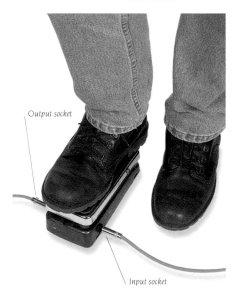

Output socket

Input socket

DISTORTION PEDALS

Fuzz and distortion effects are a fundamental part of the rock sound. While they were originally produced by overdriving valve amplifiers, there are now many different types of electronic distortion effects available as individual foot pedals. Here is a selection of widely used fuzz and distortion sounds.

Distortion

 19/2

This "Hyper Metal" foot pedal allows a controllable level of distortion to be added to the original sound. It can produce a variety of effects similar to a valve amplifier being heavily overdriven.

Boss HM-3

Fuzz Box

 19/3

The Boss "Hyper Fuzz" pedal reproduces some of the sounds of the traditional 1960s fuzz boxes. These units include the famous Sola Sound Tone-Bender and the Arbiter Fuzz-Face.

Boss FZ-2

Dual overdrive

 19/4

This pedal contains two distinct types of overdrive sound: one that is best suited to using with rhythm guitar, the other more suitable for solos. It is possible to switch between the two sounds.

Boss SD-2

Compression

 19/5

A compressor is not a distortion effect in its own right, but it is often used with fuzz and distortion effects to make the guitar sound sustain for a longer period, especially when playing a solo.

Boss CS-3

MULTIPLE EFFECTS PEDAL

Single effects pedals, such as those featured on the opposite page, are a relatively inexpensive way of changing your basic guitar sound. A major drawback of this approach is that complex set-ups involving a large number of pedals can become unwieldy. These set-ups may also make it difficult to alter settings, especially when playing on stage.

A modern solution to this problem has been the development of multiple effects modules. These are high-quality digital units, capable of producing, at the very least, reverb, delay, distortion, and compression effects. These effects can sometimes be programmed and stored via MIDI (see p. 60).

The Boss ME-10 unit shown here can chain up to 13 different effects. Up to 128 programmable patches can be stored and recalled by using the four foot pedals.

Four different multiple effect patches are described on the far right. They can also be heard on tracks 19/6 to 19/9 of the CD.

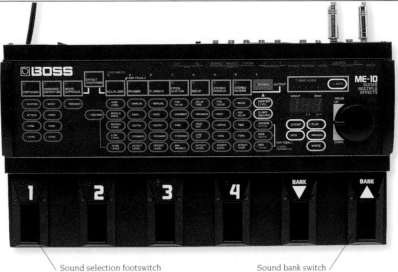

Sound selection footswitch

Sound bank switch

Reverb

 19/6

Reverb was one of the first effects to appeal to mainstream electric guitarists. It is also one of the most forgiving effects, frequently being used to mask sloppy playing skills.

Reverb and echo

 19/7

This sound combines reverb with a series of long echoes. Many guitarists have integrated echo into their playing, creating massive, layered "wall-of-sound" effects.

Multiple delay effects

 19/8

There are many different possible types of delay effect. This patch mixes reverb and delay with a pitch shift effect that replays the note an octave higher than the original sound.

Distortion and ADT

 19/9

This effect mixes a classic valve overdriven sound with reverb. Automatic double tracking has also been added to give the impression of more than one guitar sound.

Phase pedal

 19/10

Phasing effects were originally produced by recording and playing back the same signal on two tape recorders; the variations in pitch and speed produce a "whooshing" effect. Used extensively in the 1960s by psychedelic rock bands, phasing remains a popular effect. This unit dates back to the middle of the 1970s.

Electro Harmonix EH 4800

Chorus pedal

 19/11

Chorus is another popular delay-based effect. Chorus footpedals feature facilities to make minor pitch and speed variations, which can be used to create an attractive and full-bodied sound. Chorus is often used in combination with reverb and echo effects. It is also used extensively by bass guitarists.

Boss CH-1

Pitch shift pedal

 19/12

For major alterations to the pitch of a guitar signal, the original signal must be processed and appear to be replayed simultaneously with no delay. This can create problems for digital technology and can lead to a sound known as "glitching." In this example, a harmony line is created a perfect fifth above the original signal.

Boss PS-3

MIDI AND THE GUITARIST

MUSICAL INSTRUMENT Digital Interface, "MIDI," is one of the most significant technical developments to affect the guitar in recent times. MIDI was originally developed in the early 1980s as a way of allowing similarly equipped synthesizers, sequencers, and drum machines to communicate with each other. It quickly became widely used in recording, mixing, and controlling sound processing effects.

MIDI AND SOUND PROCESSING

MIDI can assist the guitarist in a variety of ways; probably the most common is as a method of controlling electronic sound processing effects. The majority of digital rack-mounted effect units are now equipped with MIDI facilities. In its simplest form, a player using a single multiple effects unit can set up a series of sound patches and select them when required by using a foot switch. Each patch may also have specific reverb, delay, compression, or distortion settings.

Switching system with MIDI

Foot pedals using MIDI, such as the Rocktron/Bradshaw unit shown below, contain a large number of "banks" of between five and ten programmable preset controls. Typically, each bank is programmed so that it contains all the sounds needed for an individual song.

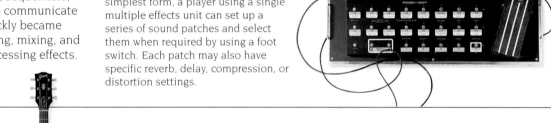

More complex systems can incorporate amplifiers that allow the pre-amplification controls, such as volume, bass, treble, and distortion, to be controlled by MIDI. The different settings can be called up by foot switch, or controlled independently by an external sequencer or computer. This kind of system is especially useful for the performing guitarist who requires a wide variety of effects during a song. Another significant advantage is that it allows the player to use exactly the same sounds for each performance without having to spend time programming them from scratch.

MIDI IN PRACTICE

Here is an example of how a guitarist might use MIDI. The foot pedal has 8 presets. Presets 1 and 2 switch between foot pedals; presets 3 to 8 control a variety of MIDI effects. The units are "daisychained" using the MIDI THRU connections. This ensures that the controlling MIDI data only comes from the original MIDI OUT on the foot switch.

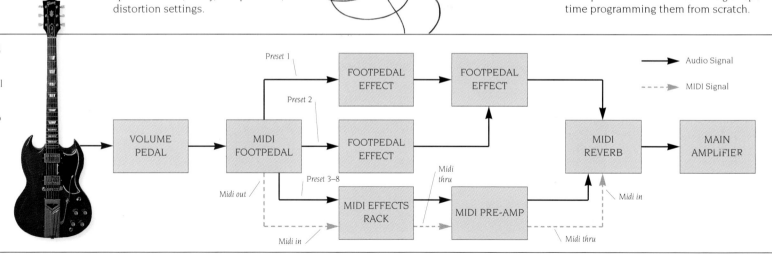

MIDI-EQUIPPED GUITARS

The MIDI guitar synthesizer allows a guitarist to play any other MIDI-equipped device. These sounds can be used in their own right or mixed with the original guitar signal. The earliest guitar synthesizers predate MIDI by many years; they were often extremely expensive and complex to use. With a few exceptions, they failed to capture the imagination of the guitarist. Equipping a guitar for use with MIDI is now a relatively inexpensive process. A MIDI pickup, which can be fitted to most guitars, is connected to a module that converts the guitar's sound waves into MIDI commands.

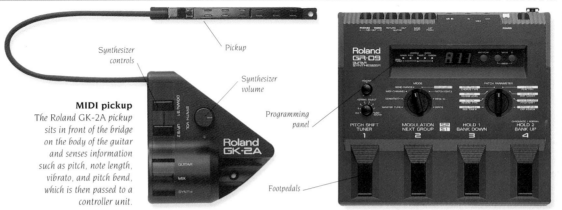

Synthesizer controls

Pickup

Synthesizer volume

Programming panel

Footpedals

MIDI pickup
The Roland GK-2A pickup sits in front of the bridge on the body of the guitar and senses information such as pitch, note length, vibrato, and pitch bend, which is then passed to a controller unit.

MIDI controller
The MIDI control unit converts the information from the pickup into MIDI data. Here the information can also be filtered so that, for example, notes played on different strings can each control a different MIDI device. Some control units, such as the Roland GR-09 shown here, are also MIDI sound modules in their own right.

USING THE MIDI GUITAR

Tracks 20/1 to 20/4 on the CD are played using a MIDI guitar system. Different strings are set to control different devices. Each track uses a different MIDI configuration. The modules used were a Roland GR-09 guitar synthesizer,

Yamaha SY77 synthesizer, Cheetah SX16 sampler, and Roland TR-909 drum machine. In some cases, the guitar signal has been mixed in with the sound. Each of the examples was played "live" – there are no overdubs.

Cheetah SX16 digital sampler

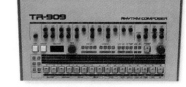

Roland TR-909 drum machine

Diagram of fingerboard and strings

	Track 1 20/1	**Track 2** 20/2	**Track 3** 20/3	**Track 4** 20/4
1	Sample (vocal)	Synth (ambient)	Synth (brass)	Synth (pluck)
2	Synth (violin)	Synth (ambient)	Synth (brass)	Synth (ambient)
3	Synth (violin)	Synth (ambient)	Synth (brass)	Sample (piano)
4	Sample (orchestra)	Synth (ambient)	Synth (brass)	Sample (piano)
5	Sample (orchestra)	Synth (ambient)	Synth (brass)	Sample (piano)
6	Synth (bass)	Drum machine	Synth (brass)	Sample (piano)

Yamaha SY77 multi-timbral synthesizer

PLAYING ON STAGE

THERE COMES A TIME when most musicians give in to the urge to perform in public. The type of equipment necessary for such an undertaking will depend on the type of music you play and the size of the venue. One thing that you will almost certainly need is a public address or "PA" system. At its most basic, a PA system could consist of an amplifier and speaker with a single microphone for vocals. On the other hand, it may feature the kind of digital effects found in a professional recording studio.

SIZE OF VENUE

The size of the venue will determine the equipment that you will need when you play on stage. For performing in a small club or bar, you might find that it is enough for each of the musicians to provide their own amplifier, which they control themselves from the stage. This leaves only the vocals to go through the PA system – drums in small venues tend to be more than loud enough without any further help. This is the kind of set-up used by most bands when they first start to perform, but it does have a major drawback: nobody is in control of the overall sound. This is likely to result in a poor sound balance between the instruments. Playing in this way, you also may not be able to hear yourself especially well, but try to resist the urge to turn your own volume up – everyone else will probably do the same thing!

In a larger or more professional venue, the PA system is likely to have more in common with recording studio technology – you are likely to find multiple speaker and amplification systems, at least one mixing desk, and rack-mounted digital effects units. The bass and guitar amplifiers and the drum kit on stage, as well as the vocalists, will usually each have their own dedicated microphones. The individual sound levels of each instrument are controlled by an engineer sitting at a mixing desk that is positioned behind the audience. In this way, the best possible sound balance can be maintained throughout a performance.

The early years
Despite having been together for over thirty years, the Rolling Stones are still one of the biggest live attractions throughout the world.

MONITORING

To allow the musicians to hear themselves sufficiently well during a performance, good PA systems usually incorporate monitoring facilities. On stage, each of the musicians has a monitor speaker on the floor in front of them from which they can hear an overall mix of the sound. Professional venues often use a separate PA system for monitoring. This consists of a mixing desk and engineer placed at the side of the stage, providing individual mixes of the overall sound tailored to the needs of each musician. For example, the vocalist might want to hear his or her voice louder than in the mix heard by the audience.

Paying dues
Being a good band is not necessarily the same as being a group of good musicians. There is no shortcut to becoming a good live act. Quite simply the more a group of musicians play together the "tighter" they will become rhythmically. The Beatles honed their skills as a band through the sheer quantity of gigs they played when they moved to Germany in the early 1960s.

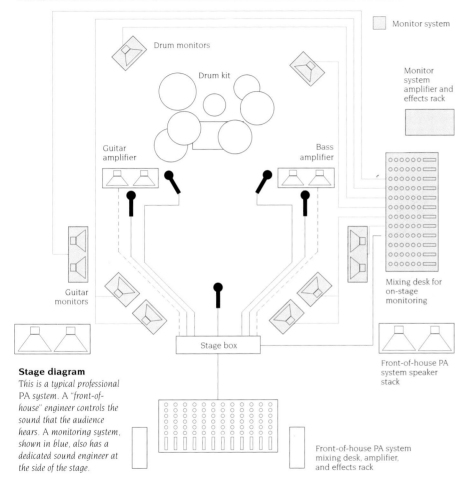

Monitor system

Drum monitors

Drum kit

Monitor system amplifier and effects rack

Guitar amplifier

Bass amplifier

Guitar monitors

Mixing desk for on-stage monitoring

Stage box

Front-of-house PA system speaker stack

Stage diagram
This is a typical professional PA system. A "front-of-house" engineer controls the sound that the audience hears. A monitoring system, shown in blue, also has a dedicated sound engineer at the side of the stage.

Front-of-house PA system mixing desk, amplifier, and effects rack

Palmer speaker simulator

DIRECT INJECTION
As an alternative to having a speaker cabinet miked up, the guitar can be plugged directly into the mixing console. This process, known as "direct injection" or "DI," has the advantage of not picking up unwanted noise, and it also prevents feedback. For many guitarists, however, the amplifier is an integral part of their sound – "DI'd" guitars can sound too clinical. To overcome this problem, a speaker simulator – a processor that simulates the sound of a speaker cabinet – can be placed between the amplifier output and the mixing desk input. In this way, guitarists can still use the tonal coloring provided by their own on-stage amplifier.

TRANSMITTER SYSTEMS
The use of radio transmitters on stage is becoming increasingly popular, even among amateur players. The system consists of two parts: a transmitter that plugs into the guitar, which is usually worn on the guitarist's belt or strap, and a VHF receiver connected to the

The transmitter is plugged into the guitar

The receiver plugs into the guitar amplifier or mixing desk

amplifier or mixing desk. This allows the player to move around the stage without having to worry about guitar leads. Radio systems can also be used in on-stage monitoring, allowing mixes to be transmitted to the performers, who can hear them using earpieces.

PLAYING SAFE
There are a number of health risks that you should always bear in mind. There is no doubt that the volume of music played in rock venues exceeds that considered safe by medical authorities, so when you are on stage, try not to get your ears too close to the loudspeakers.

Many musicians have been hurt, some fatally, when they received electric shocks. Electric shocks are invariably a result of faulty electrical equipment, often the "grounding" of a guitar or incorrect wiring. The golden rule here is to make sure that you check connecting cables, leads, plugs, and fuses at frequent intervals. Often, an amplifier will give you clues when it is becoming faulty – listen for excessive buzzing, especially when your hand comes into contact with the strings or other metal parts on the guitar. If you have any doubts at all about the electrical side of your equipment, always seek qualified help.

THE GUITARIST'S GLOSSARY

Accent – A note or chord emphasized or played at greater volume.

Acoustic guitar – Guitar designed to be played without electronic amplification.

Action – The distance between the strings and the frets on the fingerboard.

ADT – Automatic Double Tracking. An electronic effect that plays a fast single repeat to create the impression that two instruments are playing the same part.

Bottleneck – A technique for playing chords or single notes by sliding a metal or glass tube along the strings.

Bridge – The device fitted to the body of the guitar that supports and keeps the strings in place.

Capo – A clamping device fitted over the fingerboard to allow open strings to be played in other keys.

Chord – The effect of three or more notes played at the same time.

Chorus – Delay-based effect that electronically simulates more than one instrument playing the same part. Variations in pitch and time are used to create a more realistic effect.

Compression – Electronic effect that reduces the volume of loud notes, and boosts the volume of soft notes.

Damping – Technique used for muting a string. Can be used to prevent unwanted ringing or as a playing effect.

Delay – When a sound is reflected a delayed repeat, or echo, is heard. This effect is most commonly produced by an electronic digital delay line.

Distortion – Electronic effect used in rock music, where volume is boosted heavily in the pre-amp stage of the amplifier or by an external electronic effect.

Dobro – Type of acoustic guitar with built-in metal resonator to boost volume and sustain. Also known as a resonator.

Dreadnought – A large-bodied, steel-string acoustic guitar often used in country and rock music.

Electroacoustic guitar – A guitar that can be played acoustically or plugged into an external amplifier.

Feedback – A sound produced when a string or microphone picks up and re-amplifies its own signal from a loudspeaker. Sometimes used as a playing technique in rock music.

Fingerpicking – Right-hand playing technique where the strings are plucked by individual fingers.

Finger tapping – Playing technique where both left and right hands are used to fret notes on the fingerboard. Often referred to as fret tapping.

Flat-top guitar – A steel-string guitar with a flat soundboard.

Fret – Metal strips placed at intervals along the fingerboard.

Fuzz box – A pedal used to create distortion.

Guitar synthesizers – Guitars with built-in synthesizer systems for dramatically altering the sound, or those equipped with MIDI to control external synthesizers, drum machines, or processing effects.

Headstock – The uppermost part of the the guitar neck, where the machine heads are mounted.

Humbuckers – Twin-coil electronic pickups that produce a thick or "fat" sound favored by many rock guitarists.

Machine head – Mechanical device for controlling the tension, and therefore pitch, of a string. Also called a tuning head.

MIDI – Musical Instrument Digital Interface. Electronic language that allows similarly equipped devices, such as synthesizers, drum machines, sequencers, mixing desks, and sound effects, to communicate with one another.

Nut – The string support positioned at the top of the fingerboard.

Octave – An interval of 12 half steps.

PA System – Public Address System. Electronic amplification system that is used when a performer plays for an audience.

Pedals – Foot-controlled electronic units, placed between the output of the guitar and the input of the amplifier, which are used to process the sound in a variety of different ways.

Pick – Device, usually made from plastic, for striking the guitar strings. Also known as a flatpick, or plectrum.

Pickups – Electro-magnetic transducers that convert string vibration into electrical impulses, which are then amplified.

Riff – A repeated sequence of notes. Frequently used in rock music.

Scratchplate – A plastic plate fitted to the soundboard to protect the guitar body. Also known as a pick guard.

Soundboard – The front of the guitar on which the bridge is mounted.

Tempo – The speed of a piece of music.

Time signature – Symbol consisting of two numbers, placed at the start of a piece of music. It shows the number of beats, and the value of each beat, within a bar.

Tremolo – Mechanical device that can alter the pitch of a string while playing. Also a playing technique where a left-hand finger is used to create a minor fluctuation in pitch.

Truss rod – Metal rod that passes beneath the fingerboard of the guitar and reinforces the neck against string tension.

Volume pedal – Foot pedal connected between the guitar and amplifier to allow the guitarist to change volume without having to use the hands.

Wah-wah pedal – Foot-operated pedal that can be either used as a tone control or rocked back and forth to produce a "wah" sound.

CHORD DIRECTORY

THE FOLLOWING SECTION consists of a directory of chords in the keys of A, C, D, E, and G. They are probably the most commonly used keys in rock and pop music, because they form the easiest open-string chords. It is by no means a complete set of extensions, but includes those that the rock player is most likely to find useful.

USING THE CHORD DIRECTORY

Each chord is shown diagramatically, accompanied by its full and abbreviated names. The circled numbers on the chord diagram indicate which fingers you should use. Strings that have an unmarked circle indicate that the note is optional – the chord is correct using either note. Alongside the chord diagram you will find the notes that make up the chord attached to each string. Where a string is marked with an ⊗ symbol it should not be played. Next to the note names you will also find the standard music notation and guitar tablature for the chord.

On the far right of the chord diagram, in the shaded areas, you will find the guitar tablature for two additional inversions of each chord. These alternatives will allow you to play the same chords in different positions along the fingerboard.

Chord diagrams
The next ten pages contain 80 chord diagrams, in five different keys, each with two alternative inversions – 240 chord shapes in all.

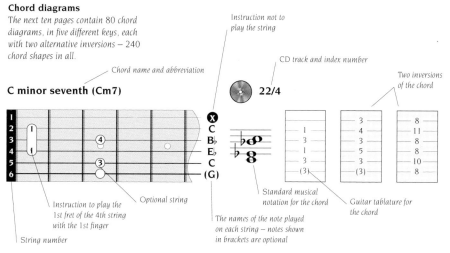

Chord name and abbreviation

C minor seventh (Cm7)

Instruction not to play the string

CD track and index number

22/4

⊗
C
B♭
E♭
C
(G)

Two inversions of the chord

Instruction to play the 1st fret of the 4th string with the 1st finger

Optional string

String number

Standard musical notation for the chord

Guitar tablature for the chord

The names of the note played on each string – notes shown in brackets are optional

LISTENING TO THE CHORDS

All of the chords in the directory can be heard on the accompanying CD (tracks 21/1 to 25/16). The CD symbol above each chord shape indicates the track and index number on the CD where you can hear the chords played. Within each index point on each track, you first hear the chord played as an arpeggio (one note at a time), then the notes played together as a chord. Many of the chord extensions have been covered earlier in the book (see pp. 30 and 34) but some of them will not be familiar to you.

If you listen to all the chord directory tracks on the CD, from the first A major chord to G thirteenth, you will quickly become familiar with the unique sound, flavor, and character of each type of chord.

AUGMENTED AND DIMINISHED CHORDS

Two of the chord extensions shown in each key – the augmented and diminished chords – have a unique feature. The notes of an augmented chord are related in such a way that moving the same basic shape three frets either way along the fingerboard produces a different inversion of the same chord. Similarly, the diminished chord shape can be moved four frets along the fingerboard to produce a different inversion of the same chord.

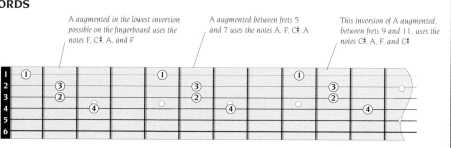

A augmented in the lowest inversion possible on the fingerboard uses the notes F, C♯, A, and F

A augmented between frets 5 and 7 uses the notes A, F, C♯, A

This inversion of A augmented, between frets 9 and 11, uses the notes C♯, A, F, and C♯

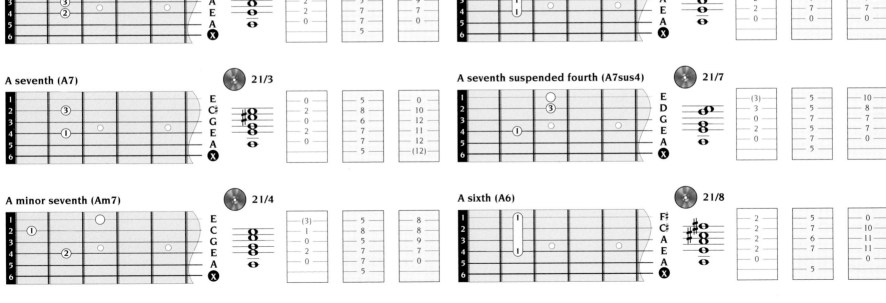

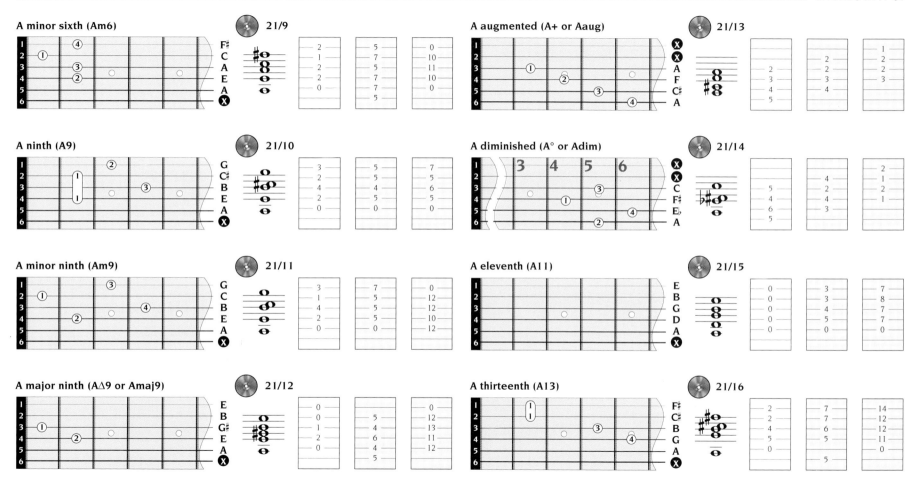

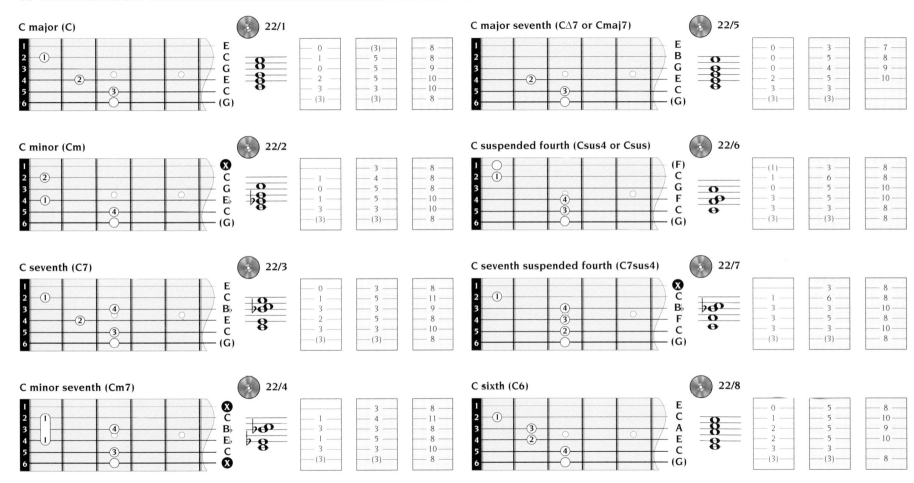

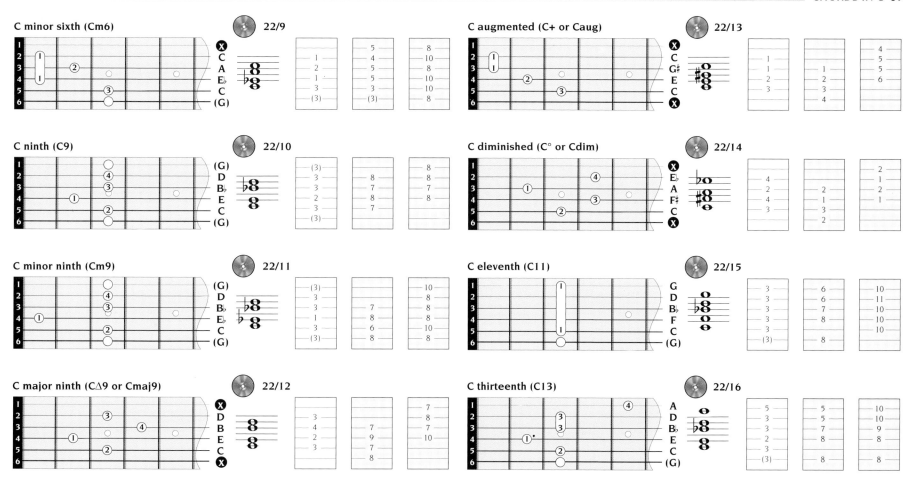

C minor sixth (Cm6) 22/9

C augmented (C+ or Caug) 22/13

C ninth (C9) 22/10

C diminished (C° or Cdim) 22/14

C minor ninth (Cm9) 22/11

C eleventh (C11) 22/15

C major ninth (C△9 or Cmaj9) 22/12

C thirteenth (C13) 22/16

D major (D)
23/1

F#
D
A
D
A
(F#)

2	(5)	10
3	7	10
2	7	11
0	7	12
0	5	12
(2)	(5)	10

D major seventh (D△7 or Dmaj7)
23/5

F#
C#
A
D
A
X

2	5	9
2	7	10
2	6	11
0	7	12
0	5	
	(5)	

D minor (Dm)
23/2

F
D
A
D
A
X

1	5	10
3	6	10
2	7	10
0	7	12
0	5	12
	(5)	10

D suspended fourth (Dsus4)
23/6

G
D
A
D
A
X

3	5	10
3	8	10
2	7	12
0	7	12
0	5	10
	(5)	10

D seventh (D7)
23/3

F#
C
A
D
A
X

2	5	10
1	7	13
2	5	11
0	7	10
0	5	12
	(5)	10

D seventh suspended fourth (D7sus4)
23/7

G
C
A
D
A
X

3	5	10
1	8	10
2	5	12
0	7	10
0	5	12
	(5)	10

D minor seventh (Dm7)
23/4

F
C
A
D
A
X

1	5	10
1	6	13
2	5	10
0	7	10
0	5	12
	(5)	10

D sixth (D6)
23/8

F#
B
A
D
A
X

2	7	10
0	7	12
2	7	11
0	7	12
0	5	
	(5)	10

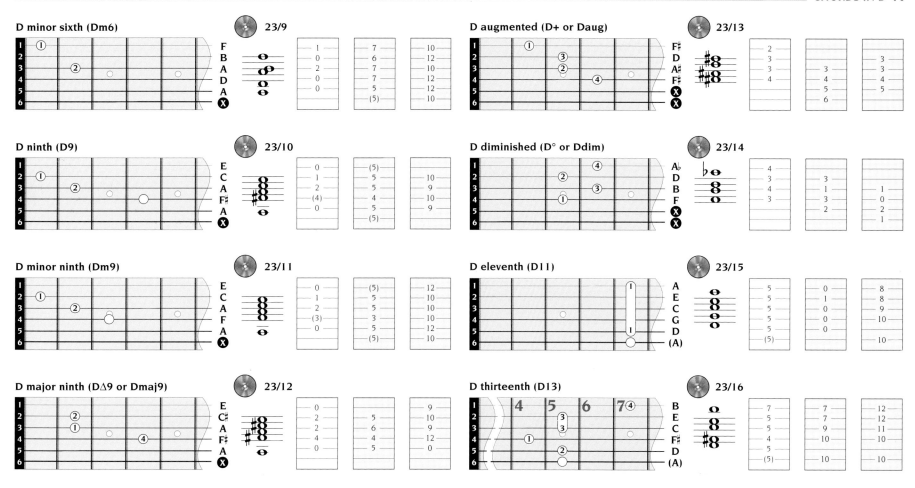

D minor sixth (Dm6) 23/9

D augmented (D+ or Daug) 23/13

D ninth (D9) 23/10

D diminished (D° or Ddim) 23/14

D minor ninth (Dm9) 23/11

D eleventh (D11) 23/15

D major ninth (DΔ9 or Dmaj9) 23/12

D thirteenth (D13) 23/16

E major (E)

24/1

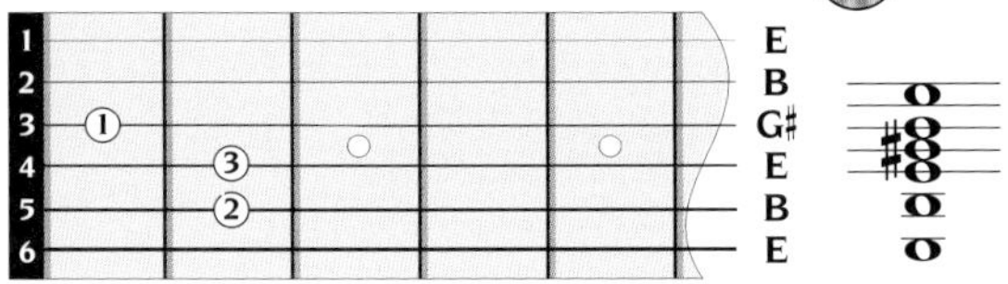

0	4	(7)
0	5	9
1	4	9
2	6	9
2	7	7
0	0	0

E major seventh (E∆7 or Emaj7)

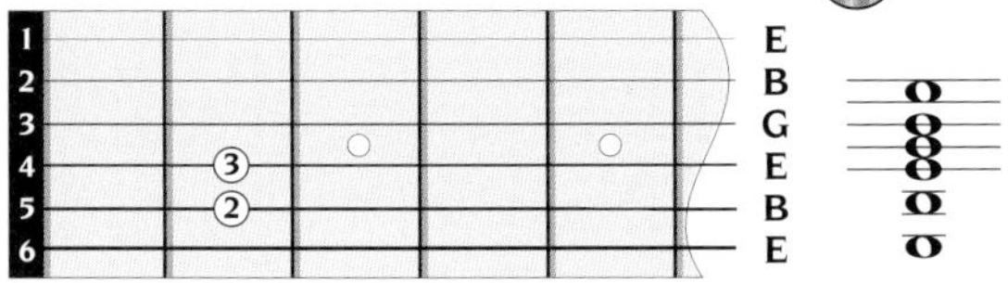

24/5

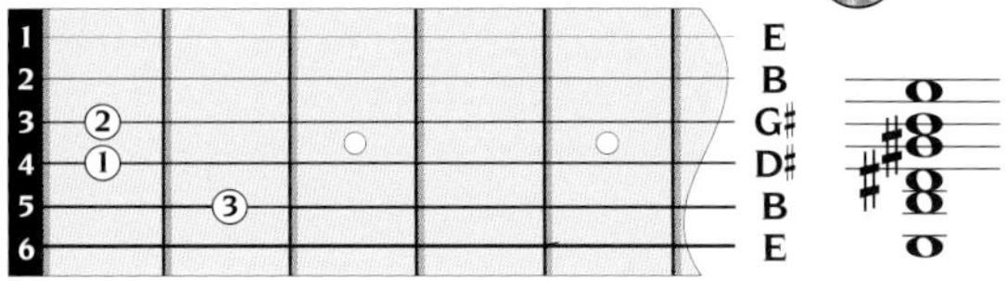

0	4	7
0	4	9
1	4	8
1	6	9
2	7	7
0	0	0

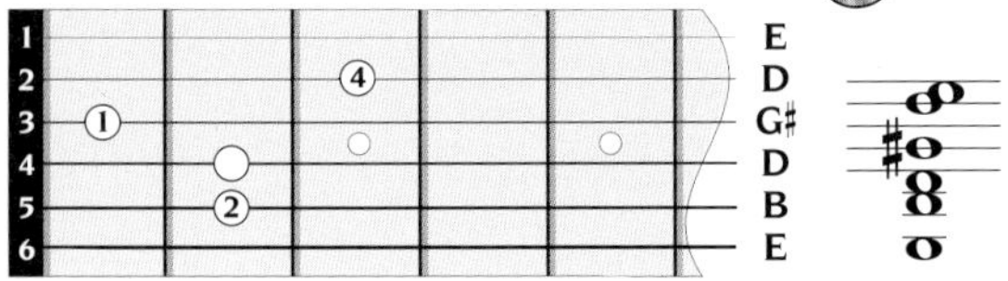

E minor (Em)

24/2

0	3	7
0	5	8
0	4	9
2	5	9
2	7	7
0	0	0

E suspended fourth (Esus4 or Esus)

24/6

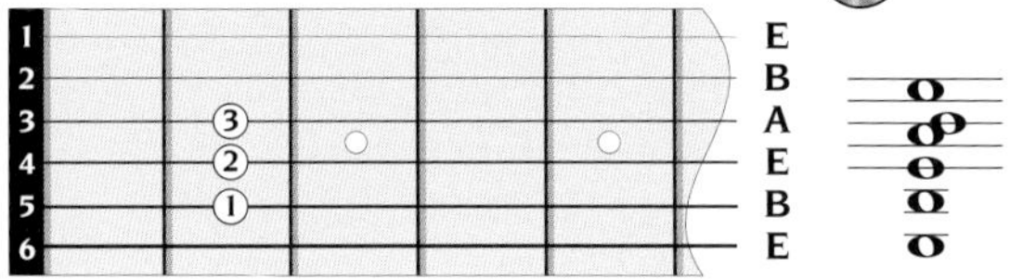

0	0	12
0	5	10
2	4	9
2	7	9
2	7	
0	0	0

E seventh (E7)

24/3

0	0	7
3	5	9
1	7	7
(2)	6	9
2	7	7
0	0	0

E seventh suspended fourth (E7sus4)

24/7

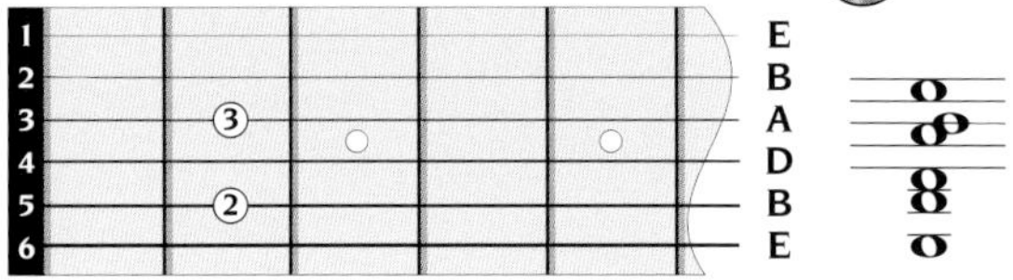

0	5	7
0	3	10
2	4	7
0	2	9
2		7
0	0	

E minor seventh (Em7)

24/4

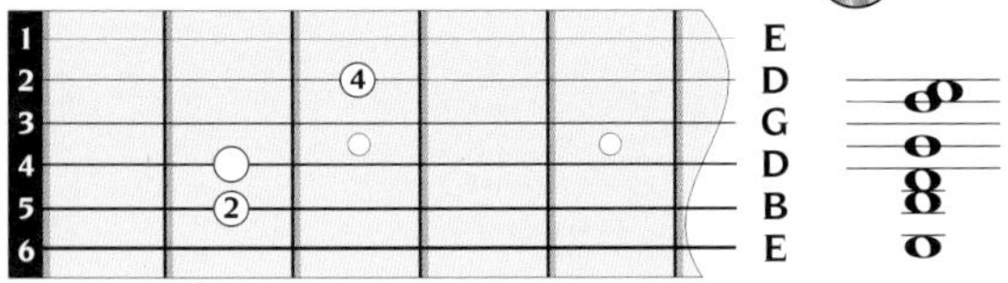

0	0	(10/7)
3	3	8
0	4	7
(2)	5	9
2		7
0	0	0

E sixth (E6)

24/8

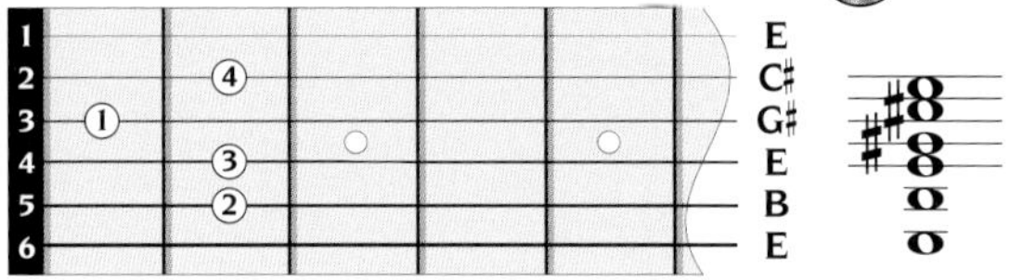

0	0	9
2	5	9
1	6	9
2	6	9
2	7	7
0	0	0

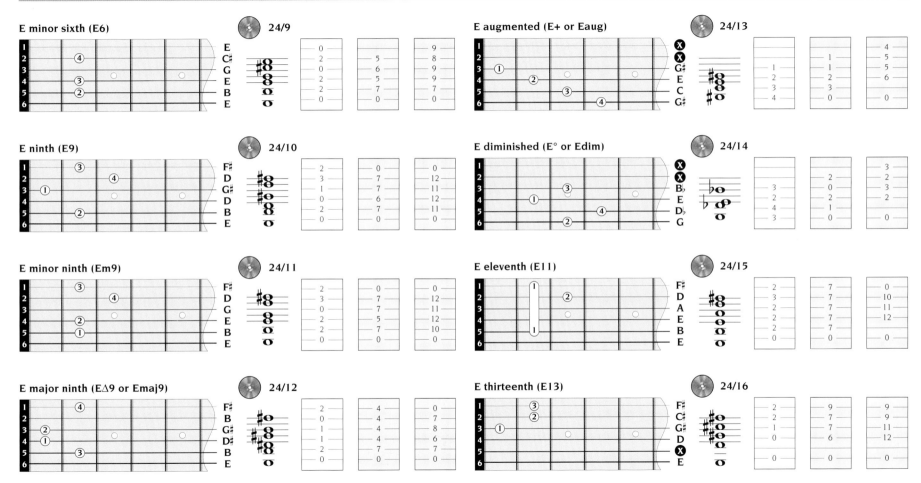

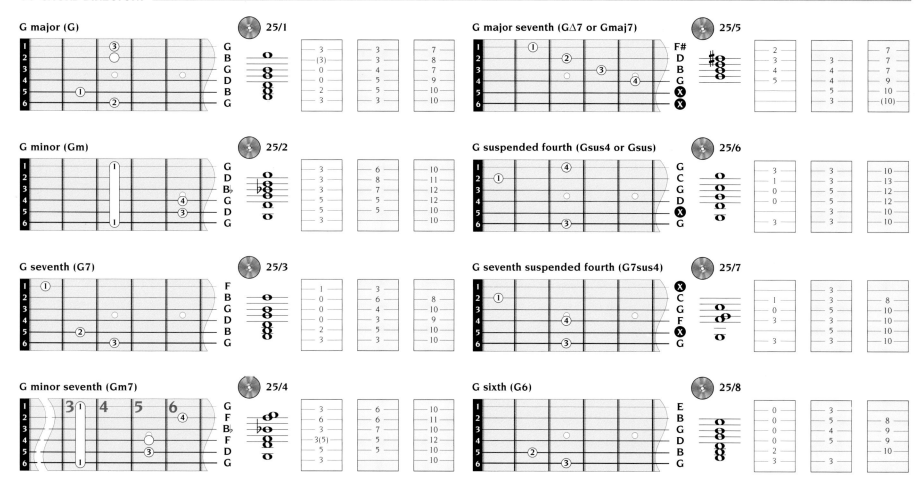

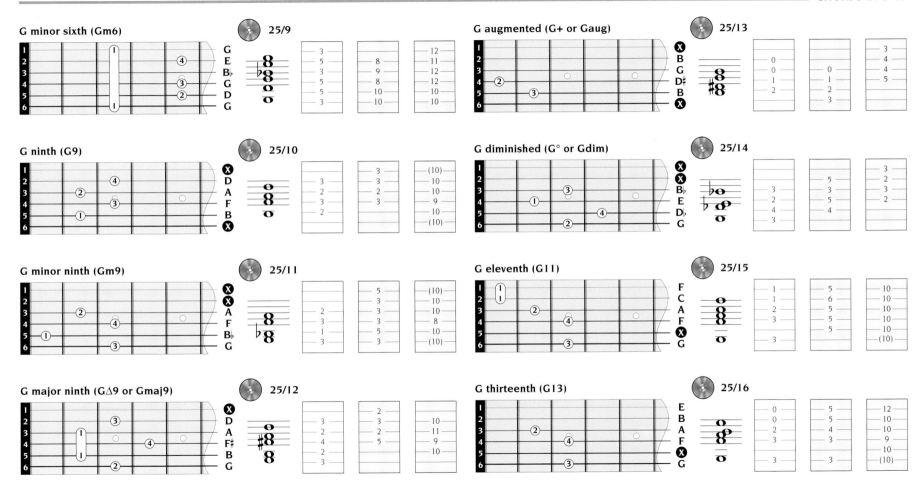

BACKING TRACKS

THE TEN BACKING TRACKS THAT you have used with some of the exercises will continue to be useful. The final pages contain a full set of chord charts for those backing tracks. They cover a broad variety of basic rock styles from simple blues boogie to a faster, complex thrash metal piece that uses multiple time signatures. You can use the backing tracks to practice or experiment with any techniques or styles that you choose. In fact, other instrumentalists or vocalists can also use them. Happy jamming!

BACKING TRACK LIST

TRACK	CD TRACK	DESCRIPTION	TEMPO	KEY
1	26/1	Grunge thrash	110 bpm	E
2	27/1	Sixties garage	150 bpm	A
3	28/1	Melodic pop	120 bpm	C
4	29/1	Slow heavy rock	100 bpm	E
5	30/1	Rock ballad	120 bpm	A
6	31/1	Rock and roll	140 bpm	G
7	32/1	Blues boogie	120 bpm	E
8	33/1	Heavy riff	150 bpm	A
9	34/1	Thrash metal	210 bpm	F♯/C♯
10	35/1	Slide blues	120 bpm	G

GRUNGE THRASH (TRACK 1)

The chords used on this slow grunge-style track are E major, A major, and D major, which are played as a repeating 16-bar sequence. The first cycle is played quietly, using right-hand damping. The second cycle is an all-out "thrash," introduced by a heavy snare beat and cymbal crash on the last beat of the previous bar. This track plays at 110 beats per minute (bpm).

26/1

SIXTIES GARAGE (TRACK 2)

This is a 1960s-style rocker. The chords used are A major, G major, D major, and C major. The track uses a 16 bar repeating sequence. The rhythm emphasizes every third eighth note in the first bar – a commonly used device in classic rock music. Try practicing notes from the minor pentatonic scales along with this track. The tempo is 150 bpm.

27/1

MELODIC POP (TRACK 3)

Songs using a standard **I-IV-V** structure are commonly found in pop and rock music. This song uses the chords C major, F major, and G major. The backing track features a "jangly" electric 12-string guitar playing the arpeggiating chords. An interesting alternative to these chords is to take a basic open-C shape and, instead of playing the F and G chords, slide the C-shape up the fingerboard to the 8th and 10th frets.

28/1

SLOW HEAVY ROCK (TRACK 4)

Suspended fourth chords are heavily used in all types of rock music. This track uses the chords Esus4, Dsus4, and A7sus4. Notice that after the introductory four bars the bass guitar no longer accompanies the chord changes but holds a continuous "throbbing" bass E beneath the chords, creating a feeling of tension. The top staff is played through four times followed by the second staff played twice.

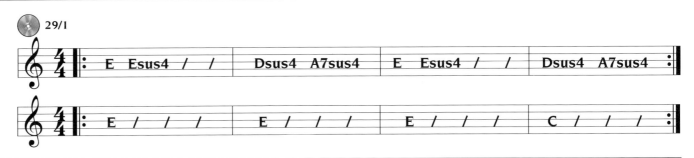

29/1

ROCK BALLAD (TRACK 5)

In this rock ballad, the verse segment (shown on the top staff) follows a classic "descending" sequence that moves from a major chord through the major seventh to the dominant seventh. The chorus (bottom staff) uses a similar device. The chords on the first beat of the the first five bars use notes that create the effect of a descent in half steps from F♯ to D. The sequence plays two verses followed by a chorus.

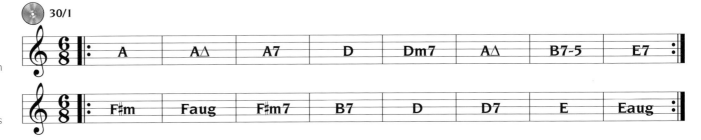

30/1

ROCK AND ROLL (TRACK 6)

The 12-bar blues cycle is still heavily used in rock music. This track features a relatively fast (140 bpm) electric rock and roll backing in the key of G. The chords used are G major, C major, and D major. Each bar contains the same type of progression – added sixth- and seventh-notes. While this style emphasizes the use of the lower strings, it is most easily played using an E-shape barre chord.

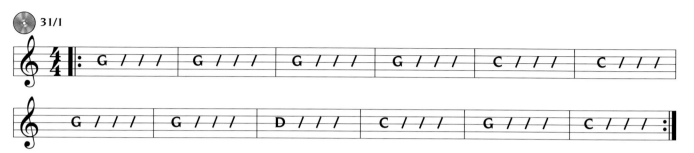

BLUES BOOGIE (TRACK 7)

This is another **I-IV-V** 12-bar blues-based backing track, this time in the key of E. The chords used are E major, A major, and B major, although these chords can also be played to great effect as dominant sevenths. Listen to the interaction of the two guitars on the CD – they have been panned in extreme stereo. Notice that they are not playing the same parts, but complementary syncopated rhythms.

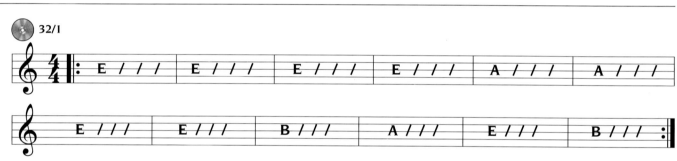

HEAVY RIFF (TRACK 8)

Rock music often relies on a guitar riff – a repeated sequence of notes – underpinned by the bass guitar playing the same notes. The chords on this track sound as if they are in A, and could be played as A major. In fact, they are C and D major chords played over a bass A. These chords can be played using an A-shape barre on the 5th fret (D), releasing the fretting fingers to play just the 1st five strings of the barre.

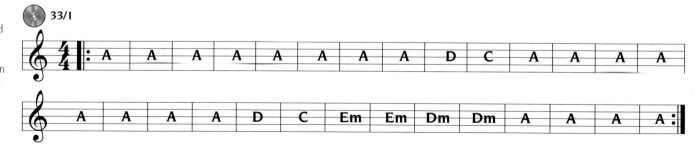

THRASH METAL (TRACK 9)

This high-speed thrash metal track uses multiple time signatures and chord sequences that are not conventionally tonal. The track begins with a twin-lead guitar riff in seven-four time, which is repeated four times (this is reprised for the bridge). The notation is shown on the right – the first part is played from the 2nd fret of the 6th string; the second-guitar harmony is played from the 8th fret of the 4th string. Sequence A switches time after six bars. Count four beats per bar – one beat for each chord played – until you reach the seventh bar, where you count in threes. Sequence B is a straightforward four-four thrash. The complete song structure is: Introduction, A, A, B, B, B, B, A, A, B, B, B, B, bridge, A, A.

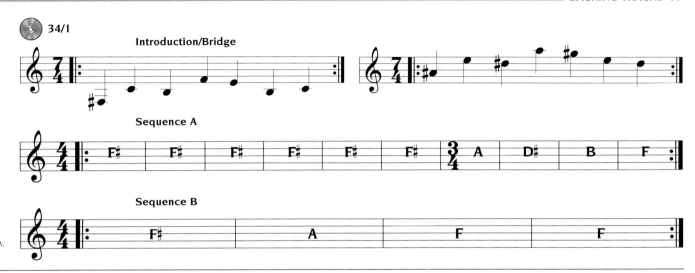

SLIDE BLUES (TRACK 10)

This final track is another blues in the key of G. The two guitars on the recording use open G tuning (see pp. 50–51). The two guitars have been panned to extremes of the stereo spectrum so that you can hear each part separately, by altering the balance on your hi-fi. The first guitar uses fingered chords, some of which are shown on page 51. The second guitar uses a slide to move up and down the fingerboard. Try playing a lead slide part to this – once again, as with all blues-based music, notes from the minor pentatonic scale are the most effective.

A DORLING KINDERSLEY BOOK

WRITTEN BY: Terry Burrows
ART EDITOR: Hugh Schermuly
EDITOR: Katie John
US EDITOR: Carolyn Clark
ASSISTANT DESIGNER: Darren Hill
SENIOR EDITOR: Stephanie Jackson
MANAGING ART EDITOR: Nigel Duffield
SENIOR MANAGING EDITOR:
Josephine Buchanan
SENIOR MANAGING ART EDITOR: Lynne Brown
DTP: Raúl López Cabello
PRODUCTION: Hilary Stephens

SERIES CONSULTANT: Jim Barber
MUSIC CONSULTANTS: Nick Kaçal,
Gilberto Dusman

MUSIC CREDITS
Original music written by Terry Burrows
℗ Dorling Kindersley Limited, London
Recorded at Piano Factory and Fair Deal
Studios, London
Compact disc produced by
The Orgone Company Ltd
ENGINEERING: Pete Giles
MUSICIANS:
Jim Barber: Guitars
Terry Burrows: Guitars, bass, and keyboards
Andy Ward: Drums and percussion

First published in Great Britain in 1995 by
Dorling Kindersley Limited,
9 Henrietta Street,
London WC2E 8PS

First American edition, 1995
10 9 8 7 6 5 4 3 2 1

Published in the United States by
Dorling Kindersley Publishing, Inc.,
95 Madison Avenue,
New York, New York 10016

Published in Great Britain by
Dorling Kindersley, Limited.
Distributed by
Houghton Mifflin Company, Boston.

LIBRARY OF CONGRESS CATALOGING-IN-PUBLICATION DATA

Play rock guitar. — 1st American
ed.
     P.   cm.   —   (Guitar tutors)
ISBN 0-7894-0189-4
1. Guitar — Methods — Self-
instruction.
2. Guitar — Methods (Rock) 3. Rock
music— Instruction and study.   I. series
MT588.P593 1995
787.8'7193166—dc20   95-11878
                                    CIP
                                        MN

Color reproduction by
Bright Arts, Hong Kong
Printed and bound by
Tien Wah Press, Singapore

PICTURE CREDITS
The Publisher would like to thank the
following for their kind permission to
reproduce their photographs:

t top; **c** center; **b** below; **l** left; **r** right.

Redferns/Mick Hutson 7bl; /John Kirk 7br;
/David Redfern 7t. Rex Features: 6br, 20bl,
62bl, 62tr; /R. Gardner 38tc; /Brian Rasic
48tr; /Richard Young 6c.

TERRY BURROWS would like to thank:
Jim Barber – whose considerable musical
skills have found their way on to recordings
by artists such as the Rolling Stones,
Mick Jagger, and Paul Rogers – for his
contributions and for his help and advice
throughout the project; Andy Ward of
Camel and Mirage fame; Armand Serra for
his thoughts on finger-tapping; Barbara
May; Dave Marshall and Ian Cullen of
Roland (UK) Ltd; Bernard Jones of
Rose-Morris; and finally, Ralph Denyer and
Richard Chapman for the groundwork laid
out in The Guitar Handbook and The
Complete Guitarist.
HUGH SCHERMULY would like to thank Nick
Buzzard for his advice and assistance.

DORLING KINDERSLEY would like to thank
Derek Mandel for checking the chords, and
Chacasta Pritlove for editorial assistance.